Picturing Fiction through Embodied Cognition

This concise volume addresses the question of whether or not language, and its structure in literary discourses, determines individuals' mental "vision," employing an innovative cross-disciplinary approach using readers' drawings of their mental imagery during reading.

The book engages in critical dialogue with the perceived wisdom in stylistics rooted in Roger Fowler's seminal work on deixis and point of view to test whether or not this theory can fully account for what readers see in their mind's eye and how they see it. The work draws on findings from a study of English and Dutch across a range of literary texts, in which participants read literary text fragments and were then asked to immediately draw representations of what they had seen envisioned. Building on the work of Fowler and more recent theoretical and empirical language-based studies in the area, Klomberg, Schilhab, and Burke argue that models from embodied cognitive science can help account for anomalies in evidence from readers' drawings, indicating new ways forward for interdisciplinary understandings of individual meaning construction in literary textual interfaces.

This book will be of interest to students and scholars in stylistics, cognitive psychology, rhetoric, and philosophy, particularly those working in the field of embodied cognition.

Bien Klomberg is a PhD candidate in the Department of Communication and Cognition at Tilburg University, the Netherlands. Her research focuses on conceptual blending and the comprehension of (dis)continuity in visual narrative sequences.

Theresa Schilhab is Associate Professor in Cognitive Biology at Danish School of Education (Aarhus University), Copenhagen, Denmark. In 2016 she achieved the higher doctorate (doctor pædagogiæ) in Educational Neuroscience on the monograph *Derived Embodiment in Abstract Language* (2017), which focuses on the biological perspective on language, and is co-editor of the anthology *The Materiality of Reading* (with S. Walker, 2020).

Michael Burke is Professor of Rhetoric at University College Roosevelt (Utrecht University), Middelburg, the Netherlands. He is the author of *Literary Reading, Cognition and Emotion: An Exploration of the Oceanic Mind* (2011) and the co-editor of *Cognitive Literary Science: Dialogues between Literature and Cognition* (with E. T. Troscianko, 2017).

Routledge Focus on Linguistics

Picturing Fiction through Embodied Cognition

Drawn Representations and Viewpoint in Literary Texts

Bien Klomberg, Theresa Schilhab, and Michael Burke

Routledge
Taylor & Francis Group

NEW YORK AND LONDON

First published 2022
by Routledge
605 Third Avenue, New York, NY 10158

and by Routledge
4 Park Square, Milton Park, Abingdon, Oxon, OX14 4RN

Routledge is an imprint of the Taylor & Francis Group, an informa business

© 2022 Bien Klomberg, Theresa Schilhab, and Michael Burke

Library of Congress Cataloging-in-Publication Data
A catalog record for this title has been requested

ISBN: 978-1-032-12589-3 (hbk)
ISBN: 978-1-032-12591-6 (pbk)
ISBN: 978-1-003-22530-0 (ebk)

DOI: 10.4324/9781003225300

Typeset in Times New Roman
by Deanta Global Publishing Services, Chennai, India

This book is dedicated to those, often discounted individuals, who regularly spend their days engaging in one of the oldest and most important forms of human communication and expression ... Drawing

Contents

Acknowledgements

We would like to express our thanks and appreciation to the team who supported us at Routledge, the Taylor & Francis Group, during the writing of this book. Primarily, we thank editorial assistant for English language and linguistics Helena Parkinson, who was based in London, and linguistics editor Elysse Preposi, who was based in New York. Without their tireless guidance, encouragement, and patience this book could not have been completed.

1 Introduction

It is sometimes said that one of the greatest felt pleasures of reading is when a good book carries one off to a fictional world; to a world, where, for a moment, you might feel that you are right beside the action or even at the centre of it. You see the scene in your mind's eye. You are "there," as it were. But in what sense are you "there"? In other words, when a person reads literature, what is that they see? Moreover, from which perspective do they see it and, further, what role or function might the written language and also personal/previous experiences play in all this? This, essentially, is what this book sets out to explore. It does so, not by means of the more traditional, reader-response approaches, but rather, by means of the creative act of drawing.

The stimulus for this book is grounded in a moment of what might be called "scientific curiosity" and it goes back to a teaching experience of one of the three authors of this book, who was teaching a guest summer course to master students in the English department at the University of Heidelberg in 2017.[1] The summer course was entitled "Language and Embodiment: Exploring the Role of Perception and Action in Language, Thinking and Memory." One of the tasks on that course was that the students had to read and critically discuss a number of contemporary research papers on the topic of language, literature, and embodied cognition. One of these papers was a study by the scholar Anežka Kuzmičová entitled "Literary Narrative and Mental Imagery: A View from Embodied Cognition," which was published in the journal *Style* in 2014. In her paper, Kuzmičová explores two important aspects of mental imagery, namely, embodiment and consciousness. In her study, she goes on to contemplate the nature of mental imagery that occurs in readers and she proposes a typology consisting of four basic variations.[2] She also briefly discusses a number of literary text fragments. One of these is by Ernest Hemingway from his novel *The Garden of Eden*. The fragment from the novel that Kuzmičová mentions in her article is reproduced below.

DOI: 10.4324/9781003225300-1

The breeze from the sea was blowing through the room and he was reading with his shoulders and the small of his back against two pillows and another folded behind his head.

While our colleague was preparing this article for critical discussion the evening before his class, on a whim of scientific curiosity, he decided to re-read the literary fragment above and then to immediately draw the scene on paper by momentarily attempting to hold the image that the text had generated in his mind's eye. In his drawing, he also included what he believed to be his "viewing point," or "perspective," of the scene. He considered the language of Ernest Hemingway in this piece to be quite straightforward. One could almost say that it read like a text that one might find in a manual. This text fragment, therefore, can be said to be very much in line with Hemingway's legendary "plain style" of writing. What our colleague had drawn, therefore, seemed to him to be quite self-evident, based on the textual description that he had in front of him. He had produced a viewpoint at approximately head height to the reader. The bed (which interestingly was not mentioned in the text) and also the reader, who was resting upright on his pillows, were to be found to the right of the tableau. The open window with the wind blowing in was situated on the opposite wall to the viewing position. Extending his scientific curiosity further, our colleague wondered whether his students would draw something similar if he asked them to take the same steps as he had taken. He hypothesized that, given that he shared many cultural and educational characteristics with his students, they probably would produce a comparable image and a broadly similar viewing point/perspective. Of course, there would be variations in the individual drawings, but, by and large, what he had drawn, and the perspective from where he had drawn it, would be generally recognizable in their sketches too if, for example, a neutral observer were to view them all and were asked to pass judgement on their general uniformity.

The day afterwards, our colleague taught his lesson as he normally would and the students discussed and debated a number of theories that were presented to them in a selection of academic research articles. One of these articles was the one by Kuzmičová, mentioned previously. However, nothing in any great detail was discussed about the Hemingway text fragment at this stage by the students. At the end of the class, our colleague asked his students to stay behind. He then took out paper and pencils and asked them to look again at the said text fragment by Hemingway. Once they had read it, they were instructed to immediately draw what they had "seen" or were still "seeing" in their imagination. They were also asked to include the point or position from which they were viewing the scene. This they could show by placing a cross, indicating the starting point of viewing, and a dotted line, representing the direction of viewing. They were given enough time to complete the drawing. Most were done within a few minutes. All were finished within ten minutes. There were just six graduate students in the group and they were all German native speakers, two male and four female. They had an excellent command of the English language as they were all English linguistics majors. After the students had finished their sketches, our colleague collected them, put them away, and told his students that he would see them again tomorrow.

That evening, he took out his own drawing and the six done by his students and arranged them on a table in front of him. We may recall at this stage that he had hypothesized that since he shared a number of cultural and educational traits with his students, and since the Hemingway text was short, plain, and descriptive in nature, there would be no major discrepancies in either what the students had drawn or from which perspective/angle the sketches had been produced. Of course, there would be some divergence, but nothing that would be irreconcilable. However, what he saw surprised him. Three of the six students had indeed drawn something similar to what he had sketched. They had also adopted a comparable viewing position to produce their drawings. However, the other three students had created widely different drawings. The viewing perspectives in these three idiosyncratic cases were equally varied and divergent.

Before we consider these, let us recall how our colleague had drawn a viewpoint at roughly head height to the reader. In this scene, the reader on his bed was to the right, resting upright on his pillows. The open window, with the wind blowing in, was situated on the opposite wall to the viewing position. The three divergent participant perspectives did not represent the scene in this way at all. The first had the viewing position on the same side as the open window, rather than it being on the opposite side. The point of viewing was placed in the middle of the window and parts of two curtains could be seen blowing in on both sides, even though, interestingly, as was the case above with the bed, there was no linguistic mention of curtains in the literary text fragment itself. The protagonist in the scene, who was seated on his bed, was now to the left of the scene rather than to the right of it. The second divergent drawing had placed the viewing position up on the ceiling in the middle of the room looking down on the event described in the text. This made it look very much like a surveyor's or architect's floorplan with very basic, flattened, barely recognizable objects in it. The viewing perspective of the third deviating drawing was perhaps the most unexpected of all. In this particular drawing, the viewing position had left the room completely. It was now outside the window, hovering above the sea and looking back into the room. This meant that there was a very limited view in the drawing of what was actually happening in the room with regard to the man in the story who was reading.

How was it possible, our colleague deliberated, that the same seemingly simplistic, descriptive text could produce such varied and deviant viewing perspectives and, as a result, lead to very different drawings created by people with broadly the same cultural and educational backgrounds? After all, the language was arguably very simple, with verbs such as "blowing" and "reading" and everyday concrete nouns, rather than abstract ones, such as "breeze," "sea," "room," "shoulders," "back," "pillows," and "head." Being a stylistician, that is, a scholar of the study language and style in literature and other texts, our colleague recalled what was, for a long time, considered to be a key text in stylistic scholarship, namely Roger Fowler's work *Linguistic Criticism* (originally published in 1986 and revised in 1996). More specifically, he recalled the following quote from that book, which has been cited and used as evidence by numerous stylisticians in their own studies over the years.

> The author's control of the reader's perception – focus, survey, and scanning of relationships – is strict, and dependent on linguistics artifices which, though unobtrusive, are clearly defamiliarizing, since the language instructs us to perceive carefully, clearly, slowly, and relevantly.
>
> (p. 165)

For a long time, this claim had been taken as a "given" to many scholars of stylistics. When our colleague reflected on those three highly divergent representations that his students had produced on that summer's day, while sitting outside by the banks of the Neckar River, and their equally divergent viewing perspectives, he had to conclude that Fowler's claim might not be as conclusive as some may still consider it to be. This assumption was backed up by his own interest in cognitive approaches to stylistics. Considered from this perspective, maybe it was not the three idiosyncratic drawings that should have caused surprise in the experimenter, but rather the three more "predictable" ones that the students produced and, also, our colleague's own drawing?

In an adjacent world to that of formal stylistics, one where cognitive stylisticians also reside, the claim of language determining what and how something is mentally apprehended has been empirically challenged during the so-called cognitive turn that occurred some 20 to 30 years ago. For example, several empirical studies by narrative psychologists have suggested that readers of literature can have very idiosyncratic reading experiences (see e.g. Miall & Kuiken, 2002; Kuiken et al., 2004; and Oatley, 2016). This has been borne out further in the work of Seilman and Larsen (1989). They discuss the role of *resonance*, or memory recall, in literary readers' personal processes of meaning construction. Furthermore, these essentially "constructivist" ideas also dominate in the field of cognitive narratology, where a focus on the interaction between the mental states of readers and narrative experiences is central (see e.g. Herman, 2014).

Arguably, the link between reading and memory goes much further back than the so-called cognitive turn in language and literature of the past few decades. In his celebrated work on reading, remembering, and schemata, Sir Frederick Bartlett showed in his empirical studies on story recall the different meaning construction processes that readers have, especially when the stories they are presented with are from an unfamiliar cultural context. More recently, work conducted by the psychologist Daniel Schacter and his colleagues (e.g. Schacter & Addis, 2007) has emphasized not just the constructive, imagery-based nature of memory, but also its simulative potential for future prediction. In light of this recent psychology-focused research, it is fair to assume that it is unlikely that literary authors have "strict control," as Fowler puts it, over the perceptions of readers through their use of language; what Fowler refers to as "linguistic artifices." Further, it is equally improbable that language, in the words of Fowler, "instructs" readers to perceive "carefully, clearly, slowly, and relevantly."

The evidence against Fowler's position that we have started to consider above in the domains of empirical reader-response studies and cognitive narratology has largely drawn on the methodological techniques of either (a) reader-response surveys and interviews or (b) linguistic and stylistic analysis. What we intend to do in our study is to go beyond the domain of language and explore whether further evidence can be found to challenge Fowler's position by means of readers' drawings. In effect, we will be investigating whether readers' drawings can provide additional evidence, in support of the "cognitive turn," to confirm or indeed deny whether readers of literary texts construct meaning in idiosyncratic ways. Therefore, we have two positions based on the way the six graduate student participants in the drawing study were split down the middle, and we can use "holding terms" to define them for now. Half the group took what might be termed an "expected" perspective to producing their drawings while the other half took what we can call an "idiosyncratic," or "unexpected," perspective. This leads to two opposing hypotheses that will be explored in the course of this book by means of manual acts of drawing. We draw on Fowler's terminology to form them and refer to them as H1 and H2, respectively.

- H1: The author's control of the reader's perception is strict and dependent on linguistic artifices
- H2: The author's control of the reader's perception is not strict and is not dependent on linguistic artifices

The study that follows is grounded in the spirit of curiosity-based science, the kind that was described at the beginning of this chapter that pertains to the language-inspired drawings of the six graduate students. This can now be considered as a kind of pre-test or focus-group test for our study that will follow. In our study, a quasi-experimental design will be employed.[3] We investigate this matter of conjectured, language-guided mental imagery with a larger group of participants. We will also have the participants in our study consider a number of literary text fragments, rather than just one, as was the case in the original pre-test. Furthermore, we will employ literary texts in two different languages, English and Dutch, in order to look, albeit at a very general level, for any divergent effects.

Even though we are minded to broadly accept the empirically proven claims that different readers construct different images during literary reading, we nonetheless seek to re-visit the claim by Fowler that language controls a reader's point of view in literary discourse processing situations. As explained above, unlike these empirical studies, which have relied on either stylistic/linguistic analysis or on reader-response interviews, we shift modalities and employ readers' drawings as a tool of analysis to explore processes of comprehension and mental imagery-formation on the basis of textual cues. We also seek to connect more fully the phenomenon of embodied cognition to the development of mental imagery that is produced by readers. Furthermore, we pay attention to differences in individual mental imagery. This, therefore, will be our distinctive contribution to ongoing research into the nature of reading-induced mental imagery.

Looking ahead to the following chapters in this book, in Chapter 2 we will define and outline the main concepts that Fowler alludes to in his citation above. These include the notions of point of view, deixis, mental imagery, and immersion. We will also look at several past studies that have relied on drawing experimentation and in particular drawing from narrative and linguistic prompts, and we will consider empirical, theoretical, and phenomenological contributions. This overview will form the basis of a theoretical framework for the study that will follow.

In Chapter 3, we present the findings from our study. We start by setting out the materials and the methods, including the set-up and the procedure of the testing. We then establish our expectations from the study and we present the data. Thereafter, we conduct a provisional discussion where we draw on point of view, language, deictic shifts, and schemas. The purpose of this interim reflection is to point forward to the main discussion to come in Chapter 5.

In Chapter 4 we go beyond the domain of language to explore embodied cognition in the domain of point of view and mental imagery. We start by summarizing how language and cognition are connected and what embodied cognition entails. We then investigate the four notions of historicity of private memories and sensory simulations, including the simulation of others' minds, meaning-making explained from the perspective of reading as a skill, and transliminality. Many of the observations that we draw on in these discussions are based on real examples that have emerged from our experimental drawing data that is presented in Chapter 3. A short provisional discussion is also conducted here.

Finally, in Chapter 5 we conduct an extended discussion in light of the data, set against the theoretical framework and the hypotheses that we have generated. Here, we explore the underlying meaning of our research outcomes, based on some of our most salient examples, and we contemplate the plausible implications of our findings. To do this satisfactorily, we revisit the claims of Fowler and also the claims that are tied to the dominant position that different readers construct idiosyncratic images when they read. We then review our hypotheses. We conclude this chapter, and indeed the book, by suggesting adjustments to both the general method and the drawing methods in our study that should be made in future scientific and scholarly explorations into drawn representations and viewpoint in literary text processing and especially in those that seek to picture fiction through embodied cognition.

Notes

1 The author in question is Michael Burke and he will henceforth be referred to in this anecdotal section of the text and later when we return to him elsewhere as "our colleague."
2 This typology and the associated concepts will be explored in greater depth in the following chapter.
3 This means a research strategy without any random assignment to control or treatment groups and without any meaningful manipulation of variables.

2   The Theoretical Framework

2.1 Introduction

In this chapter, the background concepts forming a theoretical framework are set out that will underpin the data analysis and discussions to come in the following chapters. The four main concepts that are dealt with here are point of view, deixis, mental imagery, and immersion. A fuller understanding of these will allow us to consider in greater detail the data that are presented in Chapter 3. We touch on the interconnected empirical work that has been done in the area of drawing from narrative and linguistic prompts and, in particular, in the area of writing education. We also review some more theoretical and phenomenological accounts of what it is that readers apprehend when they read literature and from what position in the experienced imagery that feat of apprehension takes place.

2.2 Point of View

Point of view has been employed extensively as an analytic tool in the field of stylistics (see e.g. Simpson, 2004, McIntyre, 2006, & Sotirova, 2006). Point of view, according to Neary (2014), is "the 'angle of telling' of a narrative – that is, the perspective from which events and/or thoughts are related" (p. 175). Neary adds that "central to the concept of narrative viewpoint is the distinction between *who tells* and *who sees*" (p. 176). This can be seen in a first-person narrative, whereby the same character, the I-narrator, both sees and tells the same events; conversely, in a third-person narration the viewer and the storyteller are separate entities (Neary, p. 176). Point of view works in a similar fashion in real life. The way a person might describe an indoor or outdoor space will depend on their spatial position/orientation in relation to the objects that are being perceived and described in that space. In addition to the spatial dimension of point of view, there is a psychological dimension. For example, the way a person feels either just before

DOI: 10.4324/9781003225300-2

or during the moment of apprehending and reporting on given objects in space can lead to what is known as a "psychological colouring" of what is seen and how it is seen. Put differently, for one viewer the glass may be half full, but for the other it is half empty. Nonetheless, it is still the same glass with the same amount of liquid in it. Returning to the idea of "who sees and who speaks," these questions go back to the ground-breaking narratological work of Genette (1980 [1972]), who first made a distinction between internal focalization and external focalization. In the case of the former "the narrator says only what a given character knows" (pp. 188–189). This focalization type is associated with first-person, homodiegetic narrators in that the narrator adopts the viewpoint of a character. External focalization, on the other hand, refers to cases in which "the narrator says less than the character knows" (pp. 188–189).

Point of view is also concerned with the notion of "worldview," or ideology. In short, every narrative viewpoint, it is claimed, has an ideological stance. Fowler (1986), based on the earlier work of Uspensky (1972), makes a distinction between three types of point of view which he calls ideological, psychological, and spatiotemporal. The first pertains to the beliefs and values through which a person perceives the world. These can be rendered in a text through the use, for example, of modal verbs and also adverbs and adjectives that take an evaluative stance. The second type, the psychological point of view, is concerned with who is the observer of the events in a narration and thus is more or less the same as focalization. The third type of point of view is spatiotemporal. On the temporal side, the focus is on three aspects: (i) ordering, as in the ordering of events in the story (such as flashbacks, flash-forwards, and narrative gaps/ellipsis), (ii) frequency (i.e. how often an event in the story is represented textually), and (iii) duration (i.e. the speed or tempo of a story, namely, the amount of textual space given to a narrative event). Most significant of all for our study is arguably the spatial, rather than temporal, notion of deixis, namely, how readers position the story not only in space, but also in time, prompted by a number of linguistic deictic markers. This is something we will turn to in our discussion in a moment. Point of view thus, in this spatiotemporal domain, directed by the arrangement of the language, might provisionally be viewed as a set of "guiding principles" that function to help readers process and understand a text. To return to Fowler, this is what he says on the matter (1996, p. 162).

The *spatial* dimension of spatio-temporal perspective corresponds to viewing position in the visual arts. Just as a painting is composed structurally so that the viewer seems to see some objects close up, some in the distance, some focused, and some less clear; so that the eye moves from one part of the painting to another in an apparently natural succession – in the same way, someone who reads a novel which represents objects, people, buildings, landscapes, etc., is led by the organization of the language to imagine them as existing in certain spatial relationships to another, and to the viewing position which he feels himself to occupy.

Arguably, such a comparison between point of view and the visual arts is not unproblematic and this appears to impede Fowler's line of reasoning that follows. The mental imagery elicited when a person is reading literature is arguably not as "direct" or as "given" as that experienced visually in the pictorial arts. If, instead, we are to accept that meaning, and its accompanying mental imagery is "constructed" (a modern, cognitive view of processing) rather than "decoded" (a more traditional, computational view of processing), then we probably have to question the visual art analogy provided by Fowler. The main reason for this is that the act of reading arguably leaves more creative and cognitive "space," as it were, for image construction to take place. This is all the more likely given that, when it comes to mental imagery, words are less constrained by the contours, colour, and context that are necessarily inherent in the form of ready-made images that are out in the world awaiting apprehension.

Moving on, a further noteworthy framework on the topic of point of view in stylistics is proposed by Simpson in his 1993 work on a modal grammar of narrative point of view. In this work, Simpson divides character point of view in two possible categories, named "A" and "B," respectively. Category A refers to first-person narrators who act as participating characters within the narrative. The narrative can be further divided into having either "positive," "neutral," or "negative" shading. These three terms can be distinguished by the level of confidence with which information is presented and the attitude or belief that is expressed through, for example, modal verbs. A positive mode of shading foregrounds "a narrator's desires, duties, obligations and opinions *vis-à-vis* events and other characters" (Simpson, 1993, p. 51). Negative shading, on the contrary, foregrounds uncertainty about events and other characters. Lastly, neutral shading is distinguished by a lack of any narratorial modality, resulting in a plain style in which events appear to be presented objectively. Category B concerns a third-person narration of a non-participating narrator. Just like category A, category B can either be in a positive, neutral, or negative shading. As the foregoing discussion shows, point of view is not an uncomplicated matter. This is best summed up in the words of Herman, Jahn and Ryan (2005) who define point of view as "the physical, psychological and ideological position in terms of which narrated situations and events are presented" (p. 442).

Within the framework of stylistics the two concepts of "modality" and "point of view" are often intrinsically linked, especially where the presentation of attitudes in a text interconnects with point of view. This is something that Gibbons and Whiteley do in their book *Contemporary Stylistics: Language, Cognition, Interpretation* (2018). The authors note how language is often imbued with the attitudes of a speaker, observing further that feelings and opinions are often commutated by means of language (p. 109). From these remarks, the role that modality plays in point of view becomes clear, as modality is one of the leading grammatical systems through which attitudes are communicated.

Modality is concerned with the stance or attitude of a speaker, writer, or narrator. Building on the work of Quirk, Greenbaum, Leech, and Svartvik (1985) and Perkins (1983), Simpson, in his earlier mentioned work, discusses four main types of modality (1993, p. 47). These are deontic modality, boulomaic modality, epistemic modality, and perception modality. The first, deontic, pertains to the notions of permission, obligation, and requirement and is captured by the use of modal auxiliary verbs in sentences like "You may go home," "You should go home," and "You must go home." The second type, boulomaic, pertains to the notion of "desire" and is portrayed by the use of modal lexical verbs in sentences such as "I hope to go home," "I wish to go home," and "I want to go home." The third type, epistemic, pertains to the notion of confidence or certainty on the part of a speaker with regard to a certain proposition and is portrayed in the sentences "I will go home" and "I shall go home." A subcategory of epistemic modality is "perception" modality. This time, instead of being about confidence in the truth of a proposition, based on knowledge, it is about confidence in the truth of a proposition based on auditory, visual, and other sensory capacities. Perception modality is expressed with the use of modal adverbs such as "evidently," "apparently," and "obviously."

If we reflect on what we have discussed so far in this theoretical section, we can see that it has not been possible to discuss point of view and modality without making mention of the system of deixis. It is to this we now turn.

2.3 Deixis

At its core, deixis is a semantic phenomenon and it is deictic linguistic devices that "index" or "indicate" that relationship. The term is derived from its Greek equivalent for "pointing or indicating" (Levinson, 1983, p. 54). Some of the earliest and most significant linguistic work on deixis was conducted by Fillmore (1975b, 1982, 1997). His Santa Cruz lectures on deixis from 1975 were particularly influential for later scholars of stylistics and other linguistic disciplines. Another influential scholar working on deixis in these early days was Lyons, who, in his work *Semantics* (1977), discussed "deixis, space and time" extensively. The system of deixis can be seen as a form of interplay between three interconnecting aspects, namely, language, contextual factors, and the individual reality of the narrator (Green, 1992). Deixis refers to the "orientational features of language which function to locate utterances in relation to speaker's viewpoints" (Simpson, 1993, p. 12). In a literary sense, it thus refers to indicators that provide the reader with the situational context that is necessary for them to be able to envision themselves within the narrative. This also relates to contextual factors, which is the second aspect. Readers are unable to perceive the referents of the text, but they "will understand these linguistic expressions as representations of the people, places, and times in the story, and will act on them as cues to imagine themselves as participating in the situation of the fictional world of the discourse" (Verdonk, 2002, p. 34). In other words, the unfamiliar context that the language describes is transformed into something identifiable as readers draw upon real-life experience and other mental frameworks. Deixis also includes the individual reality of the narrator, since labelling something as "big" or "far away" depends on the narrator's subjective ideas of these concepts.

There are three types of deictic expressions/devices, namely, place deictics, time deictics, and person deictics. Place deictics may also be referred to as spatial deictics, and "denote the relationship of objects to a speaker, which signal how a speaker is situated in physical space" (Simpson, 1993, p. 12). Simpson introduces a subdivision for spatial deixis, namely "proximal" and "distal." The former concerns a close proximity to the speaker/narrator, whereas the latter expresses the opposite. These terms not only refer to location, but also to directionality; a verb may express motion towards or away from the speaker/narrator, which is also deictic. The speaker/narrator is then the "deictic centre," or "*origo*," to or from which the action flows (Green, 1992, p. 123; Simpson, 2004, p. 30). Fowler (1996) notes that spatial deictics not only outline the spatial relations of scenes, but also order the process of a reader's perception, as these indicators guide them through the landscape, or space, in a particular manner. This is illustrated by the two following quotes.

> And as the text is organized in sequence, the reader scanning it left-to-right is led from place to place in a definite order, with a starting point, and a subsequent development, which suggest an initial viewing position, then a chain of perceptions moving from that position.
>
> (p. 164)

> The sequence offered by the relational prepositions of place is helped by some unobtrusive deictic verbs which indicate movement in a certain

direction, or a certain positioning: "ran under," "sloped from...down," "covering." Notice how "covering," a very ordinary word, implies vision from above: the observer sees the coats on top of the food.

(p. 164)

Time (or temporal) deixis "concerns the ways in which the time of the events referred to in an utterance interacts with the time of the utterance itself" (Simpson, 1993, p. 12). Tense itself can be considered deictic, with past tense corresponding to a distal perspective, and present tense to proximal perspective. Lastly, person deictics indicate relations between figures of discourse, illustrated for example by pronouns to denote particular roles (Levinson, 1983; Verdonk, 2002).

The cognitive turn has also not left deixis untouched, both in the real world of discourse participants and deixis in literary fiction. There has been much cognitive linguistics work done on how deictic expressions function in natural language situations. Diessel (2012), for example, in his work on "deixis and demonstratives," distinguishes two basic types of deixis, namely, participant deixis, with its focus on speech between participants, and object deixis, with its focus on the situational context of the discourse. Both, therefore, serve different communicative functions. Cognitive approaches to deixis in literary worlds were initially presented in a groundbreaking edited volume entitled *Deixis in Narrative: A Cognitive Science Perspective* by Duchan, Bruder, and Hewitt (1995). A guiding principle in this work is the notion of shifts in deixis, better known as "deictic shift theory." In this theory, readers create a "storyworld" into which they place themselves. What happens here is that the real-world person is "shifted" into the story, thus leading to a change in the deictic centre of the reader. The unfolding story is experienced from this location. Authors can then alter or influence the reader's deictic centre and subsequent perspective by means of a number of linguistic and narratological tools, such as a change in how speech is presented or a modification in the narrative mode. Gibbons and Whiteley (2018) define deictic shifts as "our ability to shift our cognitive stance across deictic coordinates, such as those of other speakers in conversation or into a fictional world" (p. 164). Stockwell (2002) refers to it as "a reader getting inside a literary text" and "the reader taking a cognitive stance within the mentally constructed world of the text" (pp. 46–47).

Advances in cognitive deixis have been made since the groundingbreaking work of Duchan, Bruder, and Hewitt (1995). Two models that warrant mentioning here are, first, Stockwell's description of the directionality of deixis, with his terms "push" and "pop" (Stockwell, 2002) and, second, the idea of "double deixis," put forward by Herman (1994 and 2002). Borrowed from the field of computer science, Stockwell describes a "push" as moving "down" in the text, namely, "moving from being a real reader to perceiving yourself in a textual role as implied reader or narratee, or tracking the perception of a narrator or character" (p. 47). Other examples of "pushing" into a deictic field that Stockwell notes include such literary devices as "flashbacks, dreams, plays within plays, stories told by characters, reproduced letters or diary entries inside a novel, or considering unrealized possibilities inside the minds of characters" (p. 47). By contrast, Stockwell's definition of a deictic "pop" involves moving up a level. This can be either in the text itself when a narrator interjects in a narrative or appears at the end of a story to wrap things up or it can be as you "pop" back into the world of *you*, the real reader, when you put down the book. Herman's theory of "double deixis" is embedded in the reality that pronouns can alter their reference when viewed in context; as Gibbons and Whiteley put it, "deictic projection can be inconsistent and unstable" (2018, p. 168). Of all the pronouns in English, perhaps the second-person term "you" can lead to the most volatility and unpredictability when it comes to the matter of deictic projection. Herman (1994, 2002) addresses this by categorizing the second-person uses of "you" in five different types. The first is "generalized" usage of "you" addressing a group of people. The second is fictional reference addressing a character in the text. The third is what he terms a "fictionalized" address whereby one character addresses another in the story. The fourth is a so-called apostrophic address whereby the reader in the real world is addressed. Lastly, and perhaps most interesting of all, is the so-called doubly deictic "you" (Herman, 1994, p. 381; 2002, p. 345). In this scenario, it seems that "you" has two points of reference. One of these is in the fictional world and the other is in the real world. This leads to a "blended or double form of person deixis" (2002, p. 349). With this discussion on deixis now set out, it is time to move on to discuss research conducted in the area of literary reading-induced mental imagery.

2.4 Mental Imagery

The study of mental imagery was once the domain of philosophy. Thereafter it moved to cognitive psychology and for the last 30 years it has been of fundamental interest to the field of cognitive neuroscience. Most studies in mental imagery look at the ability to recall, reactivate, and manipulate internal representations when no relevant exterior stimulus is present. These can be conscious events, like being asked to picture some object or scene, or they can be non-conscious episodes. What we are interested in in this study are mental representations or images prompted by text and immediately "secured" or "stabilized" by acts of manual drawing.

When interpreting point of view and deixis in literature, both elements can influence the perception of the scene that forms in one's mind's eye. This imagined scene has been referred to as "literary reading-induced mental imagery" (Burke, 2011). According to Scarry (2001), vivid image-making is enhanced by the skilful "instructions" of authors, by which she means that the language has to guide, or rather *instruct*, readers what to imagine. This is in some ways similar to what Fowler (1996) described and is the assumed effect of point of view. Well-written pieces of text would allow readers to perform an act of "mimesis," which nears actual perception. The theory of situation models postulates that readers construct a scene based on the situation described rather than the text itself, and that this mental reconstruction might be alike to actual experience (Rall and Harris, 2000; Zwaan, 1999). Some studies further suggest that the sensorimotor cortex becomes activated upon reading about actions in a similar way to when one actually performs such an action (Kuzmičová, 2014; Marmolejo-Ramos, Elosúa, Gygax, Madden, & Mosquera Roa, 2009; Kurby & Zacks, 2013). In this sense, mental repetitions and mental images may feel as if they are "real," as if they were elicited by actual scenes. For example, might the Hemingway text fragment presented in the previous chapter, of a man leaning against pillows reading, evoke an actual sensation of "felt reading" in the readers: a kind of double-dose of reading?

Such perceptions may even prove more versatile than they initially seem. Kuzmičová's work from 2014 attempts to categorize the mental imagery experience of literary readers according to the two axes of "embodiment" and "consciousness" as was reported in the previous chapter. She sets out four categories. The first concerns to what extent senses are involved via embodiment. Even during silent reading, the speech apparatus, auditory circuitry, and temporal voice areas would be active, meaning that there might be physiological evidence for a perceptual "voice," albeit a silent one (p. 277). Kuzmičová sees this process as applying both to verbal simulations as well as referential (visual) simulations. A reader either visualizes the literary scene in their mind's eye (referential) or experiences solely a voice (verbal). Second, the level of consciousness may vary among readers, since experiencing something and being aware that one goes through an experience are distinct. Readers can imagine scenes as images "conjured from within" (inner stance) or "conjured from without" (outer stance) (p. 281). The former is largely without any conscious effort, whereas, with the latter, the reader is aware of the mental work required. What Kuzmičová's work signifies is the plausible diversity among readers regarding literary reading-induced mental imagery. It showcases a range of possibilities for how imagination may manifest itself, supporting the question of whether the instructions of language are sufficient to universally guide readers to undergo similar experiences.

The idea of a plausible diversity among readers regarding reading-induced mental imagery, as suggested in the theoretical work of Kuzmičová above, has also been seen in the empirical data in Burke's (2011) study into literary reading, cognition, and emotion. Burke looked at the range of representations in the nature of "literary reading-induced mental imagery" in readers (pp. 56–88). One question that he posed to his respondents was: "when you read literature do you experience mental imagery?" All 18 subjects in his study responded affirmatively and nine opted to add a comment. One participant noted: "*in the sense that I sort of imagine what the people look like or where they are – not incredibly detailed though.*" Another wrote that "*it is more imagery like a feeling of faces and surroundings.*" Another reported that they experienced the imagery "*very strongly, especially when it is good writing.*" Another noted that they frequently experienced strong imagery but that often they found that "*the dialogue provokes the most images...scenery and the like usually don't give a vivid image.*" A further subject observed how descriptions that they read "*become pictures*" (Burke, 2011, p. 75).

In a later series of questions, the group was split almost fifty-fifty as to whether the mental imagery they experienced while reading literature was vivid or indistinct. A further question also pertained to *who* it was that they actually see while reading and *what* settings or locations they experience or apprehend? These responses are interesting for our current discussion on mental imagery. As such, a number of them are reproduced verbatim in the box below (language and syntax errors have been retained).

BOX 2.1

- I think that the images I make in my mind are a mix of things I remember in life. It is not that I really recognize them, but I think that this is the way the mind works. I make images I want to see and to make them I must have seen them or things that look like it or a combination of things I have experienced in life
- The surroundings are normally based on places I have been to, especially in American and British novels, because I would kind of know what it would have to look like. It totally depends on the books where these settings are of course. But mostly, if the setting would be American, I would base it on the way my home town looked when I lived there. e.g. I just read a Japanese book and the houses and alleys looked a bit American in my imagination

- Normally when reading a novel I only have a vague impression of how a character is supposed to look. The name for instance would call up a vague impression of colours, mostly. I tend to get the details wrong too. (For example, until seeing the Harry Potter film I was absolutely convinced that Draco Malfoy's hair colour was dark, like Harry's. After seeing the film, I went back to the text and found evidence that his hair really was fair all along, I just missed it)
- I never see anything while reading. Reading for me is more abstract than that. I feel, I know and I feel close to the places and persons in the book but they never mature into something physical, just an abstract experience of the narrative and the story
- If I read something that reminds me of something in my childhood for example that theme gets evoked in my head
- They are probably made up of characters and body parts of people I know. Similarly, locations are probably based on places I've been before or I have seen before in a picture or something. I think that it is impossible to not recall places or people you know or you have seen while reading literature. That is your field of reference, your experience. I should also say that I never actually see the exact faces, probably just the silhouette. Perhaps this sounds a bit far-fetched but it is almost like those pointillist paintings, where you cannot immediately see what is in the picture. You just see little parts
- I think that in visualising we tend to put emphasis on that which is known and familiar to us, both people-wise and location-wise. What we see is a mix of memories and internal knowledge about certain places and types of people
- The location and setting might have something to do with the place from my childhood, but that's all very subconscious ... when I think of a lake, I always see the same lake, unless the author describes it in detail
- Sometimes I see people who are similar to somebody I know
- I often find that when I am reading a book where people are in a certain house I actually visualise a house where I have been before, but with a lot of alterations. I've got the same thing with people and landscapes, the whole visual image is actually made up out of several pieces of people and places I've seen
- I think I take the description an author gives of a character and the scenery and then I combine that with people and places I know myself that fit into the picture to make the picture complete

- It is like dreaming, when you think you see the same thing. When you look back on dreams you see that persons and locations are composed of multiple parts. When I was younger I remember that most books I read were based in my house
- When the passage describes something that is familiar to you because you have experienced it in your childhood, you will go back to this when you need it in the novel, even if it is not specifically about your childhood in the story/passage
- I always picture the houses of friends or family when I read about houses in novels, which for me is the most peculiar thing. Also I have no idea as to why with certain novels I also picture our old house we used to live in and with others the flat my father used to live in and even sometimes my grandmother's house. I think that it is based on the descriptions from the text but I can't pinpoint what exactly
- Location and setting: very often any house or domestic setting becomes my grandmother's house and/or neighbourhood. Sometimes this mental image is so strong that I can't change it even though the novel gives clear description of locations and settings. If it doesn't fit into the picture I have of it, I will soon forget and need constant reminders (if it is something that is important somehow and recurs often). However, I will not adjust my mental image
- Fictional characters: usually remain indistinct. I know what they look like but I could not really describe them if I had to I think. If the novel turns into a movie this can sometimes collide: the character and his/her appearance are not what I imagined them to be

(data reproduced from Burke, 2011, pp. 81–83, Routledge)

In bringing this section to a conclusion we should not forget that the drawn mental imagery that we will be examining in the following chapter is grounded in what might be termed "induced" instruction. This is an important point. Indeed, had we not instructed the participants to draw what they "see" in the text, then they may not have ever seen anything at all to draw or, at best, they may have only apprehended a mere wisp of a scene rendered instantly forgettable. This may be even more so, were the reader to have been reading the entire novel in their own time and in their own space. Here, in such a natural literary discourse processing situation, the "flash" of an image could be instantaneously forgettable, located as it is in the relentless current of the continuous act of discourse processing.

An alternative to "induced" instruction is to go in search of spontaneously occurring mental imagery. In two studies, Sadoski (1983 and 1985) did just that. The experiments involved schoolchildren who read stories aloud and then completed various comprehension and recall tests. One of these included asking them if they spontaneously experienced any mental images. The subjects were not told that they would be asked about mental imagery. In the first study the subjects also saw illustrations in the test that they had to read aloud, but in the second study they only saw text without images. In the first study there was no discrimination between the illustrations that were shown and the ones recalled by the participants, but in the second study subjects reading the unillustrated stories reported nearly twice as many images.[1]

Drawing often accompanies literary writing. Authors may often sketch as they write. One theory is that writers do this "in an attempt to clarify, stabilise and make fast what they know about the appearances of people or places in a book" (Mendelsund, 2014, pp. 174–175). Mendelsund also makes a list of these authors. They include Kafka and Nabokov, who appear to have doodled extensively while writing. Other authors were skilled painters and draughtsmen and women. These included Evelyn Waugh, Edgar Allan Poe, Emily Brontë and Charlotte Brontë, and Herman Hess as well as Dostoyevsky, Goethe, Ruskin, Blake, and Victor Hugo (p. 175).

Our study therefore pertains to induced imagery. A famous study about induced imagery was conducted by Pressley (1976). He wanted his school children to remember stories better. He split his class into two groups. The treatment group was trained in making drawings to represent sentences and paragraphs and the control group was given a random task to complete. The treatment group was now referred to as the imagery group. The two groups were then asked to read the same 950-word story. The story had blank pages in between and the treatment group was encouraged to make drawings on those blank pages as they read. In a post-reading 24-item short test the imagery group outperformed the control group with no significant difference in reading times. In a similar experiment conducted by Gambrell (1982), subjects were split up and told to read in segments. One group, the imagery group, made drawings between the segments. All participants were asked, "what do you think is going to happen next?" Participants in the imagery group made twice as many accurate predictions as those in the control group. Drawing, it would seem, aids prediction. With all this in mind let us now consider the phenomenon of immersion.

2.5 Immersion

Another factor relevant to this study is the sense of "presence" within a fragment, as also brought up in Kuzmičová's 2012 work. An earlier study by Green, Brock, and Kaufman (2004) proposed that rich details about the physical environment will encourage "transportation in the narrative," but Kuzmičová (2012) and Grünbaum (2007) both argue that foregrounding the narrator's physicality stimulates the reader's imagined presence the most, thus aiding the visualization of the scene. That way, action sequences would be better suited for immersion than descriptive passages, due to references to movement and/or the physical body. Given the aforementioned evidence on the involvement of sensory and motor cortices during reading, embodiment seems a sensible encouragement for the potential of immersion (Jacobs & Willems, 2018). Empirical evidence for this idea also comes from a study on reading E.T.A. Hoffmann's *The Sandman*, showing that the imageability score of single words was the best of seven different predictors of readers' immersion ratings (Jacobs & Lüdtke, 2017). The same study also presents data suggesting that text segments classified as *action-oriented* yielded significantly higher immersion ratings than those categorized as *inner life*. In their comprehensive review of immersive processes in multiple media, Schlochtermeier, Pehrs, Kappelhoff, Kuchinke, and Jacobs (2015) concluded that the immersion potential of a medium like books is a nonlinear function of the complexity and degree of realism of the medium. As Jacobs and Lüdtke (2017) point out, the complexity dimension is determined by at least five groups of factors: (i) familiarity; (ii) heightened, unforced attention; (iii) empathy and fiction feelings; (iv) suspense, curiosity, and surprise, namely, the three universals of narrative (Sternberg, 2003); and (v) optimal descriptive or action density. These factors are integrated in the "Neurocognitive Poetics Model" of literary reading (Jacobs, 2015) which contrasts the effects of both background textual features (e.g. familiar words and situations) and foregrounding features (e.g. schemes and tropes) on immersive and aesthetic reading modes.

In another empirical study conducted by Hartung, Hagoort, and Willems (2017), the researchers wanted to discover whether personal pronouns affect immersion and arousal, as well as an appreciation of fiction. They investigated how personal pronouns influence discourse comprehension when people read fiction stories and if this has consequences for affective components like emotion during reading or appreciation of the story. They measured electrodermal activity and story immersion, while participants read literary stories with first-person and third-person pronouns referring to the protagonist. Participants in the study also rated and ranked the stories for appreciation. Their results showed that stories with first-person pronouns lead to higher immersion. Two factors in particular, namely, (a) transportation into the story world, and (b) mental imagery during reading showed higher scores for first-person as compared to third-person pronoun stories. In contrast, arousal, as measured by electrodermal activity, seemed tentatively higher for third-person pronoun stories. The two measures of appreciation were not affected by the pronoun manipulation. Their findings highlight the importance of perspective for language processing, and, additionally, they show which aspects of the narrative experience are influenced by a change in perspective.

In addition to the aspects inherent in a fragment, the language in which it is written may affect how mental imagery is constructed and experienced. This is an increasingly explored area of research. Krasny and Sadoski (2008), for example, compared whether the first or second language of bilingual students would evoke significantly different mental images and emotional responses upon reading (translated) texts. Their findings indicated that reading fragments in a second language did not hinder readers in decoding imagery or affect in literary fragments, as students handed in reports similar in content and length in both languages.

In addition to this research, many cognitive and empirical studies have taken place into narrative experiencing, idiosyncratic storyworlds, and character construction. One such line of research has been on "storyworlds" and possible selves conducted by Martinez (2018). In her study, Martinez brings together the fields of cognitive linguistics, cognitive narratology, and social psychology to argue that "storyworld possible selves" are essentially blends, which result from the process of conceptual integration of what she terms the intra-diegetic and extra-diegetic "perspectivizer." The model that Martinez builds also draws on how characters are constructed and on the social-psychological self-schema of possible selves. Such an approach permits a study of emotional responses of all kinds to narratives, thus facilitating immersive experiences.

This focus on characterization can also be found in the work of several other scholars. Two of the more prominent researchers in the area of stylistics and immersive reading experiences are Culpeper and Emmott. For example, Culpeper and Fernández-Quintanilla (2017) have researched the notion of "fictional characterization." They investigated how characters are constructed by readers between the parameters of bottom-up textual cues and top-down schematic knowledge. Their focus was on the former and they delineated three categories in characterization. These were (a) the amount of narratorial control, (b) how the self or the other is presented, and (c) to what extent the language used, i.e. the textual cue, was explicit or implicit. This led them to examine a number of stylistic linguistic mechanisms through which the narrative of the story is filtered. These include speech acts, speech and thought presentation, mind style, and point of view.

Emmott's work in this area has focused on both narrative comprehension (1997) and the interface among mind, brain, and narrative (2012). This latter work was conducted together with Sandford. Emmott says of the immersive act of reading that "in reading narrative we imagine worlds inhabited by individuals who can be assumed to behave, physically and psychologically, in ways which reflect our real-life experiences of being situated in the real world" (1997, p. 58). In Sandford and Emmott (2012), the authors go one step further to explore the psychological and neuroscientific evidence for narrative comprehension. Their research centres on the idea of how narratives, and the language used to construct them, leads to both immersion and embodiment. In their investigations they draw not just on narrative but also on rhetoric. In doing so they come back to the role that language plays in allowing readers to experience vivid fictional contexts and also how language can direct readers to construct contexts and draw inferences. The authors explore further how writers can use their creative linguistic skills to prompt different emotional and immersive states in readers. Such immersive states are at the cutting edge of cognitive stylistic and cognitive poetic research. With this in mind we now take a side-step to review drawing from linguistic prompts in the fields of academic writing and language learning, as there are important insights here that will help to illuminate our own study as it unfolds.

2.6 Drawing from Narrative Prompts

To the best of our knowledge, the way we incorporate drawing into our study of literary narrative has not been done before in research into literary discourse processing. That being said, drawing itself has been employed in diverse forms of narrative and educational research for quite a while and some of these studies warrant a brief exposition in this theoretical framework chapter. We have already reported on some drawing studies by Sadoski (1983 and 1985) and Pressley (1976) in the earlier section on mental imagery. The areas we touch on below primarily concern the field of language learning and academic writing. We also include research that has been conducted in the area of comic book research.

Seminal research into drawing and cognition was conducted by van Sommers (1984) in his book-length study into descriptive and experimental aspects of graphic production processes. In his monograph, he considers a whole range of basic executive mechanisms, including stroke-making, maintaining paper contact, and reproducing rectilinear figures and curvilinear forms. He also considers stability and evolution in children's drawings. It is a detailed work on the executive principles of simple drawing.

A crucial area where drawing has been researched is as a support to language learning in English and also as a mechanism to improve competence in academic writing. In her study, Adoniou (2012) shows how drawing can be an effective strategy for teaching writing. She started with the hypothesis that both drawing and writing draw on comparable semiotic systems and that learning is at its most effective when these two systems work together. In her study, which looked at the performance of newcomers to the English language in the Australian primary school setting, it was shown that the written quality of the test improved in those cases where the children had been drawing beforehand. This was especially the case with regard to writing informational texts. Similar results to those garnered by Adoniou had been observed already in an experiment reported in an earlier study by Caldwell and Moore (1991), in which they looked at drawing compared to discussions as a planning activity for writing. The results of their study, which employed both treatment and control groups, showed that the writing quality of the drawing group was significantly better. As such, drawing was recommended as an effective rehearsal for writing assignments in classroom settings.

Adoniou's aforementioned supposition that both drawing and writing utilize similar semiotic systems and that learning is at its most effective when these two systems work in tandem echoes the "dual coding theory" of reading and writing, as set out by Sadoski and Paivio (2001), which itself draws from work conducted at the beginning of the cognitive revolution in the 1960s and 1970s. Drawing on experimental, historical, and theoretical data from the fields of rhetoric, philosophy, education, psychology, and linguistics, the authors develop a non-computational theory that brings together reading and writing and provides a framework for literacy. Reception and production, the authors conclude, "derive from the same basic mental presentations and processes, sharing the same sources" (p. 2). At its core, dual coding theory addresses the two main symbolic systems of human cognition: language and mental imagery. It differs from previous theories in this area as "it assumes that mental representations retain properties derived from perceptions in our various sensory modalities, rather than being amodal and abstract" (p. 4).

A very different line of research that employs drawing and narrative exists in the field of visual storytelling or comic books. For example, in a recent work, Grennan (2017) sets out a theory of narrative drawing. In this novel approach, he examines the relationships between such concepts as vision, visualization, and imagination. He also reconsiders a number of linguistic-based concepts, including language, narrative, and discourse. He goes on to claim that drawings are produced in a system that embodies social behaviours. More specifically, he proposes that in visual storytelling, depictive drawing and narrative drawing are produced in an inclusive dialogic system of social action. Other research, such as the work of Cohn (2013), likewise posits that different expressions (auditory, visual, and bodily) make use of similar cognitive resources. His research reveals visual narratives (e.g. comics) to belong to a visual language, which, like spoken or sign language, includes key linguistic components of modality, meaning, and grammar. Much of his experimental work then supports the existence of general neurocognitive functions across different domains.

These examples are far from exhaustive but hopefully they have offered an insight into the range and scope of research that has been conducted into drawing from narrative prompts. In the following section we report on a phenomenological, rather than empirical, approach to understanding what it is we see when we read and how it is we see it.

2.7 Seeing While Reading

The foregoing discussion has considered "literary reading-induced mental imagery" from the perspectives of theoretical modelling and empirical, data-driven perspectives. A different methodological perspective is offered by Mendelsund (2014), who has been mentioned earlier in this chapter. We especially focus on his award-winning book *What We See When We Read*.[2] Mendelsund is a highly successful book cover designer who in *What We See When We Read* has produced an aesthetically pleasing picture book on the nature of "literary reading-induced mental imagery." His work is more like a philosophical conversation piece than a scholarly or scientific work. More specifically, it is a work on the phenomenology of reading in which conceptual design meets literary criticism, linguistics, and cognitive science. Mendelsund makes a number of observations in his book and these he orders under a collection of subheadings. Six of these sections are of interest to our ongoing study and these will be set out below. They are (i) time, (ii) vividness, (iii) co-creation, (iv) eyes, ocular vision, and media, (v) memory and fantasy, and (vi) blurredness. We will use these subheadings to order his observations.

2.7.1 Time

In his discussion on time, Mendelsund draws a distinction between "seeing" and "understanding." An example he gives is that although his understanding of a narrative will increase during the reading of a novel, this does not mean that his imagination will. Hence, by the time he reaches the end of a book the final pages are not full with "spectacle," but rather with "significance" (p. 93). He adds that not only are we picturing what we are told to see, but we are also imaging what is coming up farther down the page, so when we are reading, we are also predicting what is coming up (p. 94). He also poses a question about how much time readers spend reading sentences that they do not understand and, more importantly, what is going on in their imagination while they are being driven forward by the syntax in this semantic void? He wonders how much time we actually spend reading without understanding. Can readers produce mental imagery from sentences when they only have a basic grasp or a rudimentary flavour of its meaning? (p. 121). He also says that the author teaches him "how to imagine, as well as *when* to imagine and *how much*" (p. 125).

2.7.2 Vividness

Mendelsund has much to say on the matter of vividness in mental imagery. For example, in a discussion of Nabakov's *Lectures on Literature*, he disagrees with the author in the case of an example from Dickens's *Bleak House*. It pertains to a scene describing a cat's green eyes shown in candlelight. Nabakov makes the argument that the greater the specificity of the cat's eyes in the candlelit context of the scene, the more evocative that image will be in the reader's mind. Mendelsund disagrees, saying that although the two notions of "specificity" and "context" may add to the meaning and expressiveness of an image, they do not add to the vividness. It is the author's hard work that helps him (and indeed other readers) to understand, but not to see (p. 135). Furthermore, by the end of the novel, his delight, as a reader, is not at being able to see more vividly. Rather, it centres on his awe for the author, whose skill has allowed him to pay close attention to the world and then to render that detail in the literary discourse of his novel (p. 136). Mendelsund also asserts that more elaborate description and more attention to detail do not mean that mental imagery will necessarily be more vivid. Mental pictures will not be brought into clearer focus. The level of detail provided by a writer can determine what kind of reading experience one has (p. 143). He also challenges the notion of literary description being "additive" in mental imagery. Taking an example from reading Mark Twain, he says that by the time he has reached the words "log cabin" in the book, he has forgotten all about the previously mentioned "mist on the water."

2.7.3 Co-Creation

Mendelsund stresses the importance of the co-creation of mental imagery during reading. When we want to co-create, he says, we read and it is sketches that we want, not verisimilitude, and the reason for this is that they are ours (p. 198).[3] As an example of this, he explains that when he was a boy his family used to rent a house for the summer vacation at Cape Cod in the state of Massachusetts in the USA. That house and that location now serve to flesh out episodes in his acts of literary reading. For example, he explains how the Ramseys' summer house that is filled with guests in Virginia

Woolf's novel *To the Lighthouse* and indeed the lighthouse itself are not located in Scotland in his mental imagery (as they are in the book) but rather in Cape Cod. His childhood summer house in Cape Cod has become a "grounding image" for him. The Ramseys' house, he explains, is not a picture, but a feeling – and this feeling has primacy of the image (p. 206). He concludes this discussion by saying that readers do not picture what the author sees when writing the novel. Every narrative, he concludes "is meant to be transposed imaginatively translated, associatively translated. It is ours" (p. 207). The same thing happens, he says, when we read nonfiction. To support this he gives the example of when he reads about Stalingrad (that is, the battle that took place during the Second World War), he customizes it to his native Manhattan (p. 212). He makes a similar observation later in his work in the section entitled "Memory and Fantasy." There, he describes how, while reading about a dock in Dickens's *Our Mutual Friend*, with its boats, warehouses, and wharves, he sees the dock in his mind's eye and tries to reconstruct where it came from. He remembers a trip he took to a dock with his family when he was a child. This real-life experience is the basis for the dock that he is now seeing while reading Dickens. But this process of mnemonic transfer goes beyond fiction. It also goes beyond reading. In normal, everyday acts of conversation it also takes place. He gives the examples of how a friend of his, who has just moved to Spain, told him that he lives close to the docks… And lo and behold there, in his imagination, is the same dock from his childhood. He reflects further on how many times he has used this dock in his mental imagery, both in literary reading and in real-life situations.[4] He concludes, beguilingly, that "the act of picturing the events and trappings of fiction delivers unintended glimpses into our pasts" (p. 300).

2.7.4 *Eyes, Ocular Vision, and Media*

In this section, Mendelsund poses a question that is close to the main question that we pose in our study, namely, "when we imagine something from a book, *where* are we situated? Where is, as it were, the camera?" (p. 274). Are we jumping from camera to camera when the narrative angle of observation jumps from, say, first-person to second-person to third-person perspectives? Mendelsund contends that the choice of narrative person changes nothing visually: rather, "the narrative mode changes meaning but not angle. It doesn't change the way we see" (p. 276). He goes on to add that "our vantage point for seeing a narrative is as fluid and as unconstrained as the author's imagination in creating it. Our imaginations will roam where they will" (p. 276). Placing reading and its mental imagery into the realms of other mainstream media, he observes that "the more we are exposed to film, TV and video games, the more those types of media infect our reader perspective" (p. 277). In effect, we begin to make films and video games from and in our acts of reading. He adds that it is especially video games that have this potency for "leakage," as they "provide the participant with agency" (p. 277).

2.7.5 Memory and Fantasy

On the topic of memory and fantasy while reading, Mendelsund says that "much of our reading imagination comprises visual free association. Much of our reading imagination is untethered from the author's text... (We daydream while reading)" (p. 294). He comments further that "a novel invites our interpretative skills, but it also invites our minds to wander" (p. 294). In light of this, he concludes that the reading imagination is loosely associative – but it is not random" (p. 296). This discussion on memory also turns towards words, and he notes that words both contain meaning and provide the potential for meaning (p. 302). He adds that their effect lies not necessarily in what they semantically carry with them, but rather in "their latent potential to unlock the accumulated experience of the reader" (p. 302). He adds that words that an author uses may be dormant but they are "brimming with pertinence" (p. 303). As an example of this potential, he suggests the word "river" and concludes that it unlocks visual access to all the rivers he has seen, swam in, crossed, and sailed down, as well as seen on TV and in films.

2.7.6 Blurredness

In this final section, Mendelsund asserts that authors are curators of experiences. As such, "they filter the world's noise and out of that noise they make the purest signal they can – out of disorder they create narrative" (p. 402). He contends further that "the world, as we read it, is made of fragments. Discontinuous points – discrete and dispersed" (p. 400). He also notes that "the practice of reading feels like, and *is* like, consciousness itself: imperfect; partial; hazy; co-creative" (p. 403). This ties in with his belief that picturing stories is about "making reductions" and, through those reductions, readers create meaning (p. 415). This pictorial meaning will be blurred – it will be about the outline, not the detail (pp. 418–419).

In sum, when reviewing these sections and the phenomenological observations in them we can conclude that Mendelsund makes some engaging and stimulating points. What he claims may, on first reading, sound overtly philosophical and lacking evidence. Moreover, at times, the discourse may appear to be more art-like than science-like, but what he claims is far from vacuous or trite. If we look again at many of the theories and studies that have been set out in this chapter, we see many points of intersection and support for his observations in the embodied cognition framework. Moreover, there is also much overlap with the real participant responses that have been highlighted above in the "Mental Imagery" section pertaining to the data in Burke's (2011) study.

2.8 Conclusion

In this chapter, we have considered the background concepts that have formed the theoretical framework. These have been point of view, deixis, mental imagery, and immersion. We have also discussed some of the work that has been conducted in the field of drawing from narrative and linguistic prompts and, in particular, in the domain of writing education. We have further considered several phenomenological observations on what it is that readers might be apprehending when they read literature and from what position in the experienced imagery that feat of mental vision takes place. Having set this out here, this should now help to give meaning to our data when we discuss them in Chapter 5. We now turn to our data, which will constitute the body of the next chapter.

Notes

1 These studies are synopsized and compared in Sadoski and Paivio (2001), pp. 170–171.
2 The book is a *San Francisco Chronicle* and *Kirkus* Best Book of the Year.
3 Such "sketches" are in some ways reminiscent of aspects of the data mentioned in the earlier reported experiment by Burke (2011), for example, respondent #6, who mentioned seeing/experiencing silhouettes and pointillist-like painting representations in their literary reading induced mental imagery.
4 There are parallels here too with the data that appear in the earlier mentioned study by Burke (2011). For example, respondent #2 fleshed out the mental imagery of Japanese locations in a novel, which they had never personally experienced, with American ones, which they had encountered personally.

3   The Study

The previous chapter provided an overview of the theoretical foundation underlying the current study. To reiterate Chapter 1, this study's aim is to examine claims insisting that language instructs or dictates readers to form a particular perception in relation to developments in the field of cognitive stylistics that presume such reader perceptions to be more subjective. Consequently, it investigates two contrasting hypotheses, of which H1 states that the author's control of the reader's perception is strict and dependent on linguistic artifices, and H2 states that the author's control of the reader's perception is not strict and not dependent on linguistic artifices. To this end, we set up an informal experiment asking participants to draw the scene that they imagined upon reading a fragment and indicate the position from where they viewed this in their mind's eye. The results of this novel approach will be analysed in detail in this chapter. First, we discuss the set-up, materials, and procedure. Then, we present our analyses of the data and examples of the results and conclude with a short interim discussion.

3.1 Materials and Methods

3.1.1 Set-Up

The sample consisted of 20 students who were all native Dutch speakers. In addition, they spoke English fluently. All participants signed up for this experiment voluntarily and performed the tasks in their own time. Their ages ranged from 17 to 23 years, with a mean age of 19.8. One student was bilingual from childhood. All students attended University College Roosevelt at the time of the experiment, which is an English-speaking liberal arts and sciences honours college of Utrecht University, located in Middelburg, the Netherlands. The English-language standard of the university assured a relatively high level of English proficiency. We presented the participants with eight text fragments, which could be divided into four categories:

DOI: 10.4324/9781003225300-3

- English third-person point of view   (2 texts)
- English first-person point of view   (2 texts)
- Dutch third-person point of view   (2 texts)
- Dutch first-person point of view   (2 texts)

Within these categories, there was both a short fragment (of 2–4 lines) and a longer fragment (of 6–12 lines). All participants saw the fragments in the same order, as in the list above. So, the English cluster was as follows: third-person short fragment – third-person long fragment – first-person short fragment – first-person long fragment. The same structure was then applied to the Dutch texts. The texts were presented without any context (e.g. a title or writer) except a number above to distinguish them. To account for the possibility that some fragments are simply better suited to elicit a greater level of immersion, e.g. because of the writing style of the author, the topic, or perhaps more likeable characters or surroundings, we divided the participants into two groups. Group one received the fragments as they were originally presented, while group two received the short fragments (of 2–4 lines) manipulated to have a reversed point of view. Thus, we changed the third-person narratives into first-person narratives, and vice versa. The longer fragments (6–12 lines) remained the same. We thought it best to alter only the short narratives, as it would be easiest to maintain a nearly identical structure in just a few lines as opposed to longer texts.

3.1.2 Materials

To document the participants' drawings, we provided a drawing monitor (specifically, a Ugee, 2150). This graphic tablet allowed the participants to draw digitally so that the results could be easily recorded and saved. The software used was the drawing program Paint Tool SAI. The fragments were presented on paper, each on a separate handout. The fragments were:

1. *The Garden of Eden*, Ernest Hemingway

The breeze from the sea was blowing through the room and he was reading with his shoulders and the small of his back against two pillows and another folded behind his head.

BOX 3.1

Fragment 1 Manipulated

The breeze from the sea was blowing through the room and I was reading with my shoulders and the small of my back against two pillows and another folded behind my head.

---

2. *The Crow Road*, Iain Banks

He rested his arms on the top of the wall and looked down the fifty feet or so to the tumbling white waters. Just upstream, the river Loran piled down from the forest in a compactly furious cataract. The spray was a taste. Beneath, the river surged round the piers of the viaduct that carried the railway on towards Lochgilpead and Gallanach. A grey shape flitted silently across the view, from falls to bridge, then zoomed, turned in the air and swept into the cutting on the far bank of the river, as though it was a soft fragment of the train's steam that had momentarily lost its way and was not hurrying to catch up. He waited a moment, and the owl hooted once, from inside the dark constituency of the forest. He smiled, took a deep breath that tasted of steam and the sweet sharpness of pine resin, and then turned away, and went back to pick up his bags.

3. *Jane Eyre*, Charlotte Brontë

A breakfast-room adjoined the drawing-room, I slipped in there. It contained a bookcase: I soon possessed myself of a volume, taking care that it should be one stored with pictures. I mounted into the window-seat: gathering up my feet, I sat cross-legged, like a Turk; and, having drawn the red moreen curtain nearly close, I was shrined in double retirement.

BOX 3.2

Fragment 3 Manipulated

A breakfast-room adjoined the drawing-room, she slipped in there. It contained a bookcase: she soon possessed herself of a volume, taking care that it should be one stored with pictures. She mounted into the window-seat: gathering up her feet, she sat cross-legged, like a Turk; and, having drawn the red moreen curtain nearly close, she was shrined in double retirement.

---

4. *Farewell, My Lovely*, Raymond Chandler

Fog had come in from the ocean now, so I drove Marriott's big foreign car quite slowly. We found Purissima Canyon without difficulty. It was a quiet, lonely place in the hills behind the city. No houses, no lights. It was as dark as a midnight church. I stopped at the end of the dirt road and switched off the engine. "Stay there," I whispered to Marriott, hidden in the back of the car. "Your friends may be waiting off the road here. I'll take a look." I got out and walked along a small path down the hill. I stopped suddenly and stood in the dark, listening. Not a sound. I turned to go back to the car. Still nothing. "No one here," I whispered into the back of the car. "Could be a trick." He didn't answer. There was a quick movement just behind my head, and afterwards, I thought I may have heard the sound of the stick in the air before it hit my head. Maybe you always think that - afterwards.

5. *De Vergaderzaal*, Albert Alberts[1]

De secretaris stond bij het hoekraam van de vergaderzaal en keek naar buiten. Hij hoorde hoe achter zijn rug de concierge bezig was blocnotes en potloden over de tafel te verdelen.

BOX 3.3

Fragment 5 Manipulated

Ik stond bij het hoekraam van de vergaderzaal en keek naar buiten. Ik hoorde hoe achter mijn rug de concierge bezig was blocnotes en potloden over de tafel te verdelen.

---

6. *Karakter*, Ferdinand Bordewijk[2]

Aan het eind van de gang over zijn volle breedte liep een trap van zeven treden omhoog, zwaar beloperd, leidend naar een achttiende-eeuwse massieve deur. Die deur ging open. In het licht van een kroon met veel lampen, gesluierd door dichte sigarenrook, zag hij aan een lange groene tafel een aantal heren zitten, veel rode koppen. En aan het hoofdeinde zat een oud man met haar als van een grijze leeuw wiens manen slordig te berge zijn gerezen. Een opgewonden zware mannenstem zei driemaal achtereen, steeds de eerste lettergreep beklemtonend: "Absoluut, àbsoluut, àbsoluut."

7. *Nooit Meer Slapen*, Willem Frederik Hermans[3]

Midden op het plein staat een monument van blauw brons, een man in poolkleding op een vierkante sokkel. Hiervandaan zie ik hem op z'n rug. Wie is hij? Ik loop erheen en lees de naam die op de sokkel staat: ROALD AMUNDSEN.

BOX 3.4

Fragment 7 Manipulated

Midden op het plein staat een monument van blauw brons, een man in poolkleding op een vierkante sokkel. Hiervandaan ziet hij hem op z'n rug. Wie is hij? Alfred loopt erheen en leest de naam die op de sokkel staat: ROALD AMUNDSEN.

---

8. *Lijmen*, Willem Elsschot[4]

Ik had den man, die één tafel verder tegenover mij zat, reeds een paar keer aangekeken, want hij riep herinneringen in mij wakker, al wist ik zeker dat ik nooit met zoo iemand had omgegaan. Hij zag er voorspoedig en burgerlijk uit, als een man van zaken, en toch deed hij mij denken aan Vlaamscheleeuwen vlaggen en Guldensporenslagen, aan jongens met baarden en vilthoeden. In zijn knoopsgat zat een decoratie en naast hem, op de tafel, lagen een paar keurige handschoenen. Neen, ik had nooit omgang gehad met menschen van dat soort en toch kon ik mijn blik niet van hem afwenden. Waar, waar, waar?

The fragments were all in neutral shading, partly to be in line with Kuzmičová's (2014) study, which helped inspire this experiment (we use the same fragment by Hemingway which is also the one used in the informal curiosity-experiment conducted by our colleague in Chapter 1). Hemingway is especially famous for his plain style and the other fragments were matched to this style. This neutral shading has the most explicit mention of motor content, as it focuses on physical descriptions rather than emotions and thoughts, so this style tends to feel the most impersonal, and intuitively, relatively objective (Simpson, 1993, p. 62). Consequently, this style was considered a good starting point for this research, rather than the more modalized language of positive or negative shading. The other English texts were selected based upon course material from a stylistics course taught at University College Roosevelt, which had recommendations for works with clear neutral shading in both category A and category B (see Section 2.1) (Simpson, 1993). As for the Dutch texts, Bordewijk was selected due to his reputation of employing the plain style, which is similar to that of Hemingway. The remaining Dutch fragments were suggested by one of the paper's authors (MB) based on his knowledge of the styles of Dutch literary writers and after consulting with several of his colleagues in various Dutch literature departments.

3.1.3 Procedure

Each participant had an individual session of approximately 30 to 40 minutes, with a few outliers of 50 minutes. The experiment was conducted in the same room each time, with the same researcher present during all trials.[5] Before the actual experiment, we offered each participant the consent form and gave them instructions. The consent form listed the purpose of the study, the proceedings, possible risks and benefits, and that participation would remain anonymous and voluntary, and participants could withdraw at any time, all in line with the ethics guidelines from University College Roosevelt (where the experiment was conducted). The instructions stated that eight fragments from different novels would be presented, the first four in English and then four in Dutch. The order of fragments was identical across participants. This way, they needed to switch languages only once, which was thought to be less distracting than switching after every fragment, should we have opted to alternate the languages instead. After reading a fragment, the participants were to draw the scene that they imagined in their mind and also from where they, as a reader, had perceived this scene in their mind's eye. The instructions asked participants to indicate the actual point of viewing the scene with a symbol (like a dot or cross). Participants were also asked not to erase "mistakes," but simply correct them or start over; they were also allowed to include shifts in viewpoint if they felt that these were applicable in a given text fragment. When necessary, a small illustration was provided of how to draw the required "viewpoint," since some participants asked for an example. This illustration was only provided to resolve questions and did not resemble any of the fragments' possible depictions. There was no time limit for drawing and/or reading to avoid time pressure as a constraining factor. Still, to encourage participants to start drawing immediately after reading, the instructions stated: "After reading a fragment, draw the following (…)." They also emphasized repeatedly that the reader should draw from the mind and/or the mind's eye. After this, the researcher handed out the fragments and the experiment began. Each participant received a personal number that divided them into a particular group. Uneven participant numbers received the fragments for group one (with original fragments), while even participant numbers got those for group two (with manipulated fragments). Afterwards, we handed out a short questionnaire, in which we asked participants to indicate whether they had previously read any of the novels (a list was provided), and if so in what language, how long ago, how often, and if they remembered this during the experiment. Furthermore, we inquired whether they were familiar with the fragments in any other way, if they had any other remarks (e.g. technical difficulties), and whether they had dyslexia. For an overview of our sample group, we also asked for their age, gender, and nationality. Finally, participants were debriefed and thanked for their participation.

3.2 Results

3.2.1 Analysis Procedure

Our task asked participants to do two things: (1) draw the scene as they imagined it in their mind's eye, and (2) from where they as a reader perceived this scene. Consequently, a participant could draw a scene as if looking upon it from somewhat further away (to depict the space itself) and then still indicate, with an arrow, dot, or cross, that they perceived it from the narrator's eyes (to depict their viewpoint). As our participants were not trained in drawing techniques prior to the experiment, complex perspective drawings were not expected, and the aforementioned mismatch in scene perspective and viewing perspective was allowed. Participants were also allowed to include notes or labels to specify anything they felt was important, which are discussed in the analyses when relevant. This was another accessible way for them to clarify their intentions (e.g. regarding their own viewpoint). If the text they provided was in Dutch, we provide the translation in italics. Furthermore, all our descriptions of left and right in the analyses below are considered from the perspective of the viewer of the drawing rather than the characters depicted within it.

The following analysis will reflect the order of our instructions. First, we describe how participants drew the scene in general, including the spatial relations between the depicted entities. For each fragment (counting the manipulated fragments as separate versions), we then categorize the participants' drawings. For this, we focus on the layout of the scene, because the act of drawing forces a visual and spatial focus. Both first-person and third-person narratives present a certain "view" of a scene. Hence, a participant will need to include the entities they imagined were present and place those entities in a particular relation to other ones. Other aspects we discuss, e.g. shifts in viewpoints, are more variable and not necessarily encouraged by the fragment(s). Thus, depictions that were alike in spatial layout were grouped together, so that we could establish a "majority" interpretation. We also made "minority" subgroups for each fragment. These subgroups, which differed in number per fragment, were drawings that diverged with regard to their spatial organization. We also describe the drawings' elements in depth, including not only the features of the majority and minority groups, but also aspects appearing across those divisions. Next, we outline the second part of our instructions, namely, from where participants viewed the scene. We indicate which proportion of drawings adopted a viewpoint identical to the protagonist (shown, for example, with an arrow, cross, or other symbol originating from the head, or with the use of notes). We also indicate how many adopted a viewpoint from further away (a symbol not "attached" to the protagonist's body).

Moreover, we include examples of drawings that illustrate the occurrences discussed. For the unaltered fragments, we show an example that is representative of the majority interpretation and we also show an example of two subgroups. Since the manipulated versions are still much alike in content (and turned out to have similar "majority" interpretations), for those we provide two subgroup drawings. The images selected were representative of their group, meaning that they depict the most important spatial layout aspects characterizing that grouping. Moreover, the selection was clearly drawn, meaning that they showed an immediately recognizable depiction, a not too complex numeration of shifts in scenes, or not too many (overlapping) lines, arrows, or textual cues. This way, the drawings function as illustrative, interpretable examples in this chapter.

3.2.2 The Data

3.2.2.1 Fragment 1: The Garden of Eden *(Ernest Hemingway)*

BOX 3.5

Fragment 1

The breeze from the sea was blowing through the room and he was reading with his shoulders and the small of his back against two pillows and another folded behind his head.

Five out of ten participants drew a similar scene and thus formed the majority interpretation. In short, they depicted the protagonist near the window, which was on an opposing or connecting wall, so that the view outside was visible for the protagonist. Of those five, four created a drawing highly similar to what our colleague had done for this fragment, as described in Chapter 1. One exactly followed this description and drew the protagonist on a bed to the right of the room, with the window on an opposing wall (see Figure 3.1). They indicated wind blowing into the room with wiggly lines. The second drawing was very closely related, with the only difference being that the window was on a connecting wall rather than an opposing one; here they also drew curtains waving in the wind. The remaining two just

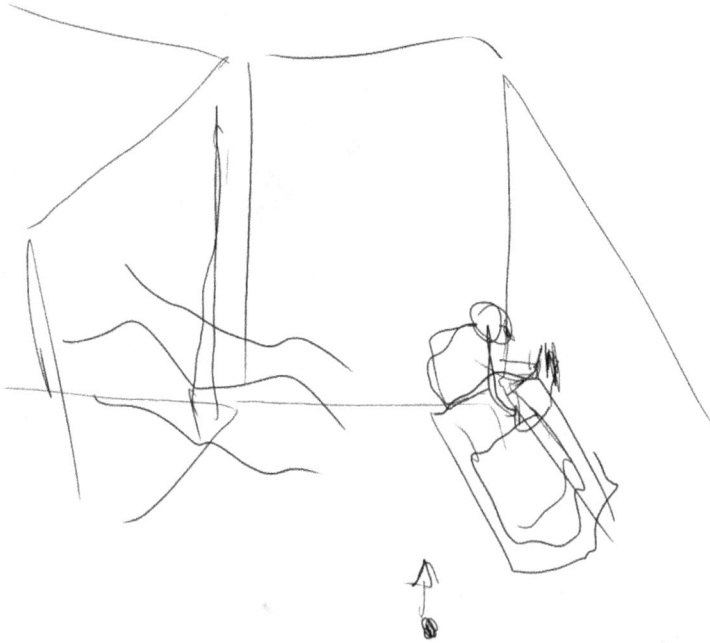

Figure 3.1 Majority interpretation

had their drawing mirrored, with the protagonists (one on a bed, one on a couch) to the left of the room, and the window on the opposing wall to the right. One of them included static curtains and wind blowing inside. The fifth participant of this group was similar to this general layout, but drew no walls. Instead, they had the protagonist on a bed on the left of the canvas, both seen from the side. There was a desk (facing the front) to the right of it. The open window was next to that, and seemingly placed on the same wall as the long side of the bed was pushed against. The lack of walls leaves it more ambiguous as to where the window is in relation to the bed; perhaps it was intended as being opposite the bed, but the participant did not know how to draw this. Nevertheless, the immediate impression remains that the window is on a connecting wall, which aligns with the rest of this majority interpretation. Out of these five participants discussed so far, four of them drew wavy lines in the window to represent the sea outside.

The first subgroup consisted of four drawings that presented the house or room that the protagonist was in from somewhat further away and included the sea outside not through the window, but next to the house/room (see

Figure 3.2 First subgroup interpretation

Figure 3.2). For three of them, the sea was on the left of the drawing (e.g. Figure 3.2), with a transparent depiction of a house or room (one participant drew no outer walls) to the right of the page. Then there was a window where the wall was (or would be), and inside sat the protagonist (see Figure 3.2). One participant drew the protagonist on a bed, another on a chair, and one on the ground, but all included the pillows that were mentioned in the text. Two included wavy lines to indicate wind. The final participant in this subgroup flipped this general layout. She/he drew the sea on the right of the page, and a transparent house (on stilts) on the left side, with the protagonist on the floor resting against pillows. Like the others, they indicated wind, but they were the only ones to draw clothes for the protagonist, a plant inside of the house, and birds outside. All four participants included a house or room in their drawings and positioned the protagonist facing the window.

The second subgroup was formed by one drawing that had the protagonist in a chair on the right side of the room, facing forward to the viewer (Figure 3.3). The window was on the same wall as the one that the chair was resting against, to the left. This differed from the window being on an opposing or connecting wall (or no wall), since the protagonist could easily look outside in all those previous cases. In this case, that was impossible. Here, too, the sea could be seen through the window.

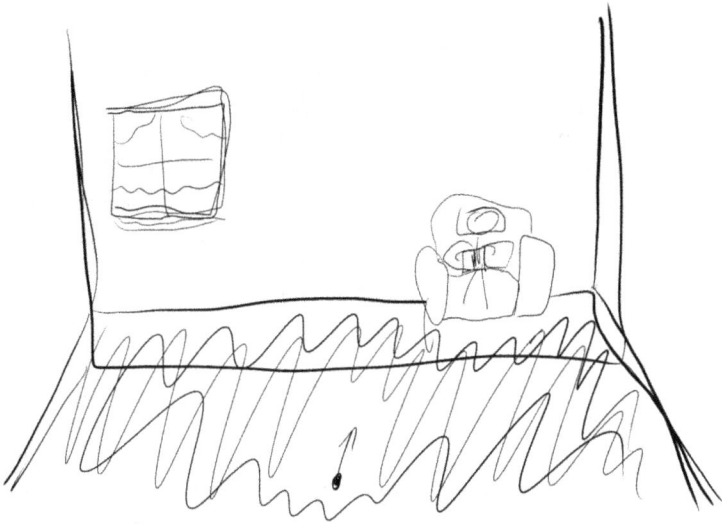

Figure 3.3 Second subgroup interpretation

Out of all drawings in total, only one participant did not draw a book in the hands of the protagonist. Seven drew the described pillows and four drew the breeze explicitly (either through wavy lines like in Figure 3.1 or via dynamic curtains in one case). Five drew a view of the sea through the window, while the four in the last subgroup drew the sea independently (see Figure 3.2).

Regarding perceived viewpoint, nine out of ten participants perceived this scene from somewhat further away, as indicated by an eye or arrows, as for example in Figures 3.1 and 3.3. The one participant who indicated sharing the perspective of the protagonist is shown in Figure 3.2.

3.2.2.2 *Fragment 1 Manipulated:* The Garden of Eden *(Ernest Hemingway)*

BOX 3.6

Fragment 1 Manipulated

The breeze from the sea was blowing through the room and I was reading with my shoulders and the small of my back against two pillows and another folded behind my head.

Six out of ten participants drew a similar scene and constituted the majority interpretation. Here again, this meant the protagonist was seated somewhere in the room with the window either on an opposing or connecting wall, and could look outside the window from where they sat. From these six, one had the protagonist leaning against pillows on a bed to the left of the canvas and the window on the opposing wall to the right. This participant also drew a lamp and a carpet, as well as curly lines to indicate wind (labelled "sea breeze"). Of the remaining five, one had the window on a connecting wall, with the protagonist on a bed to the left of the page and the window more to the right. Four others then drew no walls, but the window seemed to be on a connecting wall as well. One included a bed with pillows (and wavy lines for wind), and another one had the protagonist sitting on the ground (with pillows); this latter participant also included curtains, wind, and a door. The final two of this majority group then used window seats rather than beds or pillows. Like the other drawings in this group, one placed the protagonist on the left side of the page, with the window more towards the right. There were pillows behind their back(s), propped up against a straight line labelled "the corner of the room," curtains, and a view of the sea and the beach. In this majority group, four others also included the sea through the window. The other window seat drawing diverged slightly, in that the protagonist did not face to the right side of the canvas, as the rest had done thus far, but the left. Instead, the depiction showed a large, rectangular window, separated by panes, with the protagonist seated up against pillows on the right of the window seat. One window was open.

The first subgroup here then differed in that the protagonist could not easily look outside. One drawing had the participant in a chair with pillows seen from the side. This chair was placed partly in front of the window (seen from the front), so that the window was mostly left of the protagonist. Therefore, while in other drawings the window was to the right, and thus seemingly in front of the protagonist's face, in this drawing the window was near the back of the protagonist's head. Additionally, wavy lines were drawn to represent wind. The second drawing showed a large, rounded window separated by panes, with the protagonist's pillows leaning against the window itself (Figure 3.4). This again was a window seat. This protagonist was facing the bottom of the page, so similarly, the protagonist would have to turn around to witness the view (which here was showing the sea).

The final subgroup then consisted of two more divergent drawings. One included a shift between the outside and the inside, drawing two separate scenes. The first showed the sea and a lighthouse, and the second the protagonist on a couch pushed against the wall on the left of this scene, underneath a window with curtains. The other drawing was from a bird's-eye

Figure 3.4 First subgroup interpretation; notations read (from left to right) "pillows," "human reading," and "I visualize it as I'm sitting with my back towards the window"

view perspective (see Figure 3.5), depicting the sea on the left side. Curled lines resembling wind go towards a straight line in the middle (presumably, the wall of the house) with ultimately to the right side of the page the protagonist, lying on their back on a rectangular shaped piece of furniture with presumably a pillow (a round shape beneath their shoulder). This was then also the only drawing to not include a window or a book.

Out of all drawings, all ten included the described pillows and nine included the implied book. One of them, Figure 3.4, was ambiguous whether a visual book was shown, but the notes specified the act of reading. Six then showed the sea through the window, while two showed the sea outside independently (the last subgroup). Half of the ten drawings explicitly illustrated a breeze by including wavy lines (see Figure 3.5).

Regarding perceived viewpoint, six out of ten participants viewed the scene from further away, as exemplified in Figure 3.5 with an arrow. Out of those six, two included a shift in scenes. One is described above as first showing the outside scene (the lighthouse) and then the inside. The other participant also first imagined the outside, but did not draw two scenes; rather, they wrote a note ("outside, then inside into bed"). Seemingly, they were looking outside the window first, as they indicated their first perceived viewpoint (labelled with a "1") near there. The second perceived viewpoint

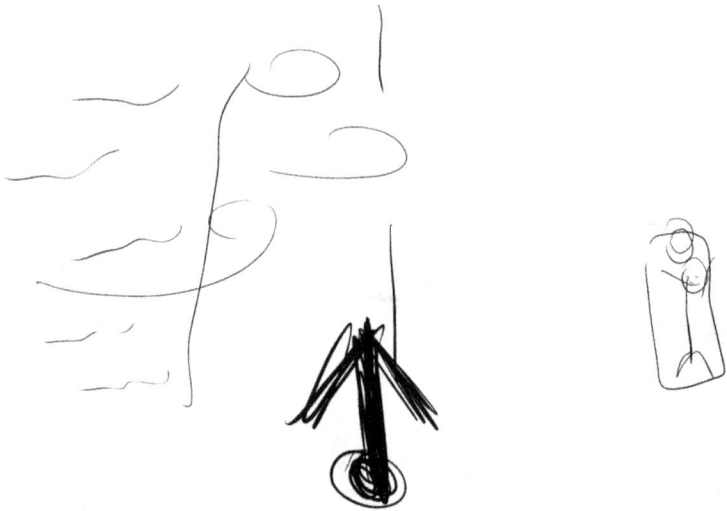

Figure 3.5 Second subgroup interpretation

(labelled "2") then focused on the book the protagonist held, and the third (a circle, labelled "3") encompassed the entirety of the protagonist's body on the bed. Four participants adopted the narrator's viewpoint, as exemplified in Figure 3.4 (indicated by the arrow and further clarified through text, see caption).

3.2.2.3 Fragment 2: The Crow Road *(Iain Banks)*

BOX 3.7

Fragment 2

He rested his arms on the top of the wall and looked down the fifty feet or so to the tumbling white waters. Just upstream, the river Loran piled down from the forest in a compactly furious cataract. The spray was a taste. Beneath, the river surged round the piers of the viaduct that carried the railway on towards Lochgilpead and Gallanach. A grey shape flitted silently across the view, from falls to bridge, then zoomed, turned in the air and swept into the cutting on the far bank of the river, as though it was a soft fragment of the train's steam that had momentarily lost its way and was not hurrying to catch up. He waited a moment, and the owl hooted once, from inside the dark constituency of the forest. He smiled, took a deep breath that tasted of steam and the sweet sharpness of pine resin, and then turned away, and went back to pick up his bags.

Nine out of 20 drawings formed a majority interpretation together, as all showed the protagonist standing in front of the wall of the bridge and looking down towards the view (see Figure 3.6). There were variations in how much background was included. Two drawings were from relatively far away, showing the protagonist on the bridge as a small figure. One drew the trees to the left of the page, a river running diagonally across the page (from bottom left to top right) with, on top of it, a bridge with the protagonist. Underneath the bridge (going towards bottom right) were many lines bundled together, presumably representing the train's smoke, since there were also clouds drawn at the bottom of the page. Alongside the entire right side

Figure 3.6 Majority interpretation; notations read (from left to right) "forest," "from above," and "river"

of the canvas (top to bottom) were the train tracks. The other participant from these two "far-away" interpretations drew multiple scenes; in the first one, the train tracks were to the left of the scene, parallel to the river that had the bridge (including the protagonist) perpendicular to it. The trees were on the right side of this scene. The second scene showed the protagonist looking down from behind, so only the waves of the river were visible above the bridge. The third replicated the first scene again, just now with a train on the tracks. Other participants in this majority group had their scenes closer by. For two, the entire body of the protagonist was visible, standing in front of the wall but with less background. From left to right, one of them drew the forest, waterfall, viaduct, and river, while the other had the forest on both sides of the page, with a waterfall and river in the middle. Neither of these included train tracks. Even closer by were three drawings that included just the upper body (in one case) or just the head of the protagonist (in two cases). The former included the background in separate scenes. Thus, after their first scene showing only the protagonist's back, their second scene portrayed a train going from left to right on the page, crossing a river that ran from the bottom left to the top right of the canvas amidst a forest. The third scene was a part of a tree with an owl in it, and, fourth, the protagonist (seen from the front) walking towards two suitcases. Regarding the other participants drawing the protagonist's head up close, they had the protagonist looking down at the river, which was a relatively horizontal stroke on the page (see Figure 3.6). One had the forest above that (Figure 3.6), while the other had the forest only in the top left corner, and the train tracks vertically in the middle (thus crossing the river). This person also included a "grey shape," as mentioned in the fragment. The final two drawings of this majority interpretation zoomed in even more, drawing only the arms of the protagonist, as it would look when one would look down upon themselves while leaning on a wall. Both had the river again as relatively horizontal strokes across the page. One included trees in the top left corner, with the train tracks horizontally in the top right, disappearing behind the trees. This person also included a bird in the top right corner. The second participant had the train tracks on the left so they crossed the river and the trees on the right side of the page, obscuring the river. This person as well included a "grey shape."

The first subgroup included eight drawings, which displayed the protagonist and the bridge predominantly from the side (see Figure 3.7). Six of them had those elements on the left side of the page, with some minor variations. Three included trees in the top left corner of the page, with the river then moving from there (high up) to the right bottom side of the page (which was in most cases evidently lower down). One of those three included just the train tracks on the bottom left, but the other two also added the viaduct and the train itself, including puffs of smoke. One also added the grey shape

Look at it from far away, big scene

Figure 3.7 First subgroup interpretation; notation reads "look at it from far away, big scene"

mentioned in the fragment (labelled as such with a note). Another re-created the same scene a second time to depict the protagonist turning away from the view. Similar to this layout was a participant who drew the river rather horizontally and parallel to the train tracks above it (see Figure 3.7). The trees were on the right side of the page and partly obscured an incoming train. They also included mountains in the background. The fifth participant of the six that had the protagonist on the left side of the canvas, placed the trees in the middle of the page, with the river passing in front of it, but originating not from the left side but from the right side, as this participant placed the waterfall on the right of the canvas. This drawing also included black spirals drawn in front of the trees, representing the smoke of the train. The sixth participant drew the river aligned vertically on the page, with the bridge (from a side view) across it. The remaining two participants of this subgroup just had their drawings flipped, with the protagonist on the right side of the page. One had the river horizontally, with above it the via-duct and train, placed in the middle of the page, with the trees and an owl (labelled as such) on the far left. The other also had the trees on the far left, but the train tracks and river were shown as diagonally crossing lines.

The final subgroup then drew the scene at approximately head height to the protagonist, seeing them from the front rather than the back or side (see

Figure 3.8). One flipped the view around in a separate scene to show the back of the protagonist and the background, namely a horizontally aligned river, with above it the viaduct and train, and above that the forest. Then they flipped back to viewing the front of the protagonist and outer wall of the bridge. The others kept to one scene. Figure 3.8 shows an example, where the river flowed beneath the bridge from bottom left to top right, with a forest in the top right corner and the train underneath the bridge. Moreover, this example included the "grey shape," "bags," "owl," and "mountains" (all labelled). The other single scene portrayed the river as a horizontal stroke, with directly above it the bridge, aligned with the river. The forest was in the top left (behind the bridge) and the train tracks in the top right.

Overall, all 20 depicted something resembling a forest and a river. Most often, this forest was portrayed as stereotypical trees (meaning, cloud-like circles to denote leaves or circle-shaped scribbles), but six participants drew the typical shape of pine trees (meaning, resembling a general triangle shape). One participant switched between forest types across the two scenes they drew. Their first scene had the label "deciduous forest" with a matching illustration, while the second scene labelled the forest "coniferous forest" with now a pine tree illustration. Seemingly, these two forests were in the

Figure 3.8 Second subgroup interpretation; notations read (from left to right) "watching from above, this perspective," "grey shape," "train," "dude," "Loran," "bags," "mountains," and "owl"

same place, so possibly this participant just changed their mind. One other of those six drawing coniferous forests specified they were "pine trees" with a label. Regarding the other elements, 13 included the railroad (meaning, tracks were visible), and seven a train. Eight included steam, so there could also be steam without a train in sight. Nine included either a viaduct and/or waterfall; these two often went hand in hand. Seven participants illustrated an owl or bird, and one indicated through a note that there was the "sound of [an] owl." Four showed the grey shape mentioned in the fragment (often labelled as such for clarity), and six included bags near the protagonist.

Concerning the perceived viewpoint from where participants viewed the scene, 14 out of 20 participants viewed it from further away (see Figures 3.6–3.8). Six participants viewed it from the narrator's eyes, most noticeable when participants only drew the arms of the narrator. One of these included shifts in viewpoint that focused on the view, and the final one was above the narrator's head. Still, as they started out from the narrator's eyes and maintained that perspective through a number of shifts, they were counted as using that perspective predominantly. In total, nine participants drew shifts, mostly following the train tracks, the owl, and the river. The other 11 presented a static scene.

3.2.2.4 Fragment 3: Jane Eyre *(Charlotte Brontë)*

BOX 3.8

Fragment 3

A breakfast-room adjoined the drawing-room, I slipped in there. It contained a bookcase: I soon possessed myself of a volume, taking care that it should be one stored with pictures. I mounted into the window-seat: gathering up my feet, I sat cross-legged, like a Turk; and, having drawn the red moreen curtain nearly close, I was shrined in double retirement.

The majority interpretation was formed by six drawings all depicting the protagonist reading in front of or next to the window, with the bookcase in the same room. Half of these protagonists were seated in chairs either partly in front of the window or right next to it (see Figure 3.9). One of these three drawings used a bird's-eye view. This drawing, and one other, placed the window on a vertical wall on the left side of the canvas, with the protagonist next to or in front of the window, and the bookcase then on the connecting (horizontal) wall to the right. Out of these two, one also included an easel with a "drawing" (labelled as such) to the left of the bookcase. The bird's-eye view drawing included a sun outside and a table and chairs across the protagonist. The other half of the protagonists were seated in the described window seats. One of these drawings again used a bird's-eye view, but only partly. Their first scene is seen from above, like a map, showing the protagonist moving through one room into the other with a dotted line. This room included a table and chairs too. The second and third scenes then exit a bird's-eye view and show the window seat from the front, including the protagonist and a number of pillows. In total (out of all six), four depictions had a table and chairs, one of which was only visible through a doorway. The others were all included in the same room as the protagonist. Similar to this second bird's-eye view drawing, three more depictions had the window and protagonist approximately in the middle of the page. Out of this total of four drawings placing the window in the middle, two drew the bookcase on connecting walls (one on the wall on the left side and one on the right side). One other participant had the bookcase opposing the window, and one more had it placed against the same wall as the window. Within this majority group, four drawings had explicit doors, placed either across the bookcase (in one case), on the same wall (one case), or on a connecting wall (two cases).

The subgroup was formed by four drawings where it was ambiguous whether the bookcase and the window seat were in the same room or in separate places. One included only the legs of the protagonist sitting cross-legged in front of the window, with a book in their lap (see Figure 3.10).

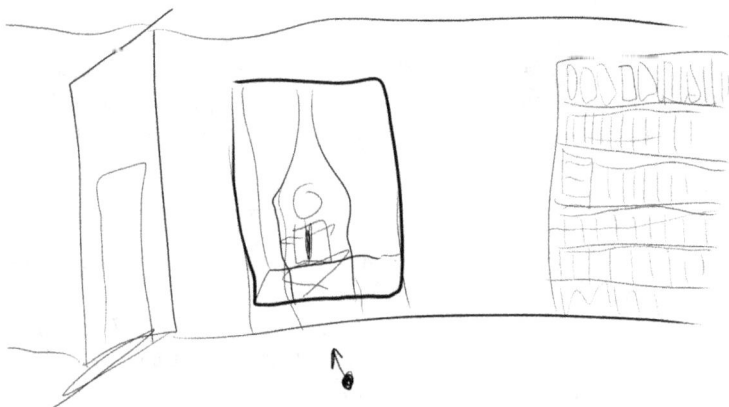

Figure 3.9 Majority interpretation

This perspective mirrored the view one would have looking down upon their own legs when seated. Moreover, there were pictures in the book and a sun outside. Two other drawings in this subgroup were similar to each other in layout and in their number of scenes. Namely, they first drew the bookcase; one of them included a protagonist in front of it, while the other did not. As a second scene, one drew the protagonist sitting in front of a window with curtains, seen from the front. The other instead did the same as the previous drawing: they drew just the legs of the protagonist in the window seat, as if looking down upon themselves. The final drawing in this subgroup depicted at least two rooms (see Figure 3.11). The first included just a table and a lamp. With dotted lines, the participant showed an arrow going through the door on the right of that room into the second room they drew. This one included just the bookcase seen from the front, and a window on the connecting wall to the right. This window seemed to be above a door. The dotted arrow continued in this room and went towards this door. Yet, a circle was drawn around the window high up on the wall, and a third scene to the right side of the page shows the protagonist in a window seat reading a book, with trees visible through the window. Seemingly, the window in the room with the bookcase is the one that the protagonist is

Figure 3.10 Subgroup interpretation first example; notation reads "viewing from the person's eyes"

Figure 3.11 Subgroup interpretation second example; notation reads "bookcase"

seated against, yet this window is drawn impossibly high if one wants to lean against it. Possibly, the participant meant for the window seat to be a different window after all. Therefore, this drawing was included in the ambiguous subgroup.

All ten drawings drew the protagonist sitting cross-legged (see Figures 3.9–3.11). Only one depiction did not include curtains and one other did not include a bookcase (the one showing only the legs of the protagonist). Eight out of ten did visualize the book in the hands of the protagonist. Seven drawings included the described window seat (see Figures 3.9–3.11), while three opted for chairs. Lastly, five participants made it explicit there were at least two rooms by showing it in another scene or including a door (one adding a note "door to breakfast room") or a doorway one could look through to see a table and chair. Two implied a second room but were ambiguous in whether it actually was separate or the same space as the other scene.

Regarding perceived perspective, six out of ten participants viewed the scene from further away (see Figure 3.9). They all looked upon the protagonist from somewhere inside the room, watching their face. One clarified that they viewed it from the door opening. From the four that adopted the narrator's perspective, two showed this by drawing only the legs of the protagonist (Figure 3.10), looking down upon them as they would upon themselves when sitting. The other two clearly placed the arrow or dot on the protagonist's head (Figure 3.11). One appeared to merge with the narrator, as they coloured in the protagonist's head and labelled it "me."

3.2.2.5 Fragment 3 Manipulated: Jane Eyre *(Charlotte Brontë)*

BOX 3.9

Fragment 3 Manipulated

A breakfast-room adjoined the drawing-room, she slipped in there. It contained a bookcase: she soon possessed herself of a volume, taking care that it should be one stored with pictures. She mounted into the window-seat: gathering up her feet, she sat cross-legged, like a Turk; and, having drawn the red moreen curtain nearly close, she was shrined in double retirement.

Here too the majority interpretation was formed by five depictions showing the bookcase, the window seat, and the protagonist in the same room. Noticeably, here there were all clear window seats. Three of them drew the previous room the protagonist was in as well, which included in two cases a breakfast table set with plates and cutlery (one of which also decorated the room with a lamp, cabinet, and a painting on the wall). The other case wrote down that there was a "big desk," a "desk lamp," and "squishy chairs." One participant drew just one room (seemingly) and indicated it on the bottom as the "drawing room." However, next to the table and chairs in the middle of the room they wrote "breakfast room." Either they referred to this section within the room as another room, possibly by mistake, or they visualized the middle part as a separate room. This remains ambiguous. The last of these five participants just drew the room with the bookcase. Regarding this room, three out of the total five drawings had the window on the right side of the page. For two of them, the bookcase was on a connecting wall on the left, while the other had the bookcase on the same wall. Two of these three had a table across the window. The remaining two participants within this majority interpretation had the window on the left side of the page, with the bookcase on the right, either on the same wall (with a table across it) or on a connecting wall. Furthermore, the two participants who did not include tables in that room instead included an easel in there, either with a drawing on there (as the participant wrote beside it) or with paintbrushes next to it. There was another participant notating that there was a "pillow" in the window seat, and there were "little table [and] chairs" across it. Another detail is that two scenes also included the sun shining through the window. Lastly, one participant of this majority interpretation group also included a zoomed in version of the scene, showing only the book that the protagonist was reading. Presumably, they imagined this book through the protagonist's eyes.

The first subgroup could be made up of three drawings, where it was again ambiguous whether the bookcase and the window seat were in the same space. One drawing showed just the one scene, viewing the protagonist on their back, on what could both be a window seat or a couch, with, in the background, an indication of a bookcase, but possibly seen through a window or a door. Thus, it remained ambiguous whether there was a bookcase and/or window included here. The other two ambiguous ones included multiple, seemingly independent scenes, both very similar (see Figure 3.12). In both cases, the first scene showed the protagonist in the breakfast room, with a table with plates on it. One of them included two people seating at opposite ends at the table, with a closed door in front of that, while the other included a view through the doorway (Figure 3.12), which seemed to show the bookcase in the next room. The second scene, in both cases, then showed the protagonist from the side (facing left), picking a book from the bookcase next to them or behind them. Figure 3.12 then included a scene of the protagonist climbing onto the window seat, which the other participant did not have. The last scene for both showed the protagonist, seen from the front, holding a book and sitting in the window seat.

The second subgroup, consisting of one drawing, clearly indicated separate rooms in two separate scenes. This participant showed the bookcase on

Figure 3.12 First subgroup interpretation; notations read (from left to right) "window," "climbing up," and "reader" (to indicate that the black dots are the origin of the reader's/participant's viewpoint)

the left wall, with the protagonist in front of it, a table and chairs in the middle of the room, and a door on the wall on the right side. The second scene then showed the protagonist from the front, holding a book and sitting in the window seat, similar to most of the previous subgroup.

The final subgroup then was made up of one drawing as well (see Figure 3.13), depicting no window at all. On the left side of the page was a bookcase, then a table, and then a door that was open. Partly obscured by the open door was the protagonist in a dress, seen from the side.

Across all drawings, nine clearly depicted the bookcase and one drawing remained ambiguous. Namely, it was not clear whether this object was seen through a door or a window, and was thus a bookcase or a building outside. Eight protagonists sat in a recognizable window seat and eight of them held a book (not all of these overlapped). One participant indicated that the protagonist was holding a "drawing," and that there was an "open book with pictures" lying beside them. Eight participants clearly sat cross-legged (see Figure 3.12), and one remained ambiguous. One protagonist remained standing (Figure 3.13). There were seven instances of curtains. Lastly, there were eight drawings indicating the presence of a second room, through either doors, doorways that could be looked through, or two scenes in separate rooms.

Then for the perceived viewpoint, seven out of ten participants viewed this scene from somewhat further away (see Figures 3.12 and 3.13). The

Figure 3.13 Second subgroup interpretation; notation reads "from side" (to indicate the origin of the participant's viewpoint)

participant drawing only the book, as if looking down upon it from the narrator's eyes (viewing the content) was presumed to share the narrator's eyes. Two others had arrows originating clearly from the eyes of the narrator.

3.2.2.6 *Fragment 4:* Farewell, My Lovely *(Raymond Chandler)*

BOX 3.10

Fragment 4

Fog had come in from the ocean now, so I drove Marriott's big foreign car quite slowly. We found Purissima Canyon without difficulty. It was a quiet, lonely place in the hills behind the city. No houses, no lights. It was as dark as a midnight church. I stopped at the end of the dirt road and switched off the engine. "Stay there," I whispered to Marriott, hidden in the back of the car. "Your friends may be waiting off the road here. I'll take a look." I got out and walked along a small path down the hill. I stopped suddenly and stood in the dark, listening. Not a sound. I turned to go back to the car. Still nothing. "No one here," I whispered into the back of the car. "Could be a trick." He didn't answer. There was a quick movement just behind my head, and afterwards, I thought I may have heard the sound of the stick in the air before it hit my head. Maybe you always think that – afterwards.

Ten depictions formed the majority interpretation, all showing the car and the protagonist getting out of the car to walk around (see Figure 3.14). Five of those showed the fragment in four scenes, which two divided into the protagonist in the car, getting out to walk a little bit, getting back to the car, and getting attacked. The other two (see Figure 3.14) started from viewing the car from the outside, then viewing a scene in the car, seeing the protagonist walk outside of the car, and getting back to it. The final one then mixed those previous approaches and viewed first the car from the outside, then the car's window to hear the characters talk, the protagonist walking on the road, and the stick hitting the protagonist. The remaining five depictions in this majority group were as follows: two drawings included just two scenes, one drawing included three scenes, one had six, and the last one nine. Regarding the first of the two-scene drawings, it showed the car on the left side of the canvas, following a horizontal road that swerved off towards a city behind a hill in the top-right corner. It then showed the road on the left side of the page with the car on the right, and in the middle was

Figure 3.14 Majority interpretation; notation reads "inside of car"

the attacker hitting the protagonist, who was facing the car, with a stick. The other two-scene drawing had the road diagonally across the page (bottom left to top right), with the car driving along it towards the right. In the back were hills and behind them the ocean. The second scene then had the car to the right and the protagonist in the middle, looking out towards the hill and ocean. The third scene drawing showed the car from a bird's-eye view, with an almost vertical road and an ocean and beach on the left of the page. Then the car was parked on the far right and the protagonist was on a road, with the ocean and beach still to the left. Next, from within the car, between the chairs, one saw the protagonist getting hit with a stick through the back window. The six-scene participant drew the first scene almost identically, also from a bird's-eye view. They first watched the ocean, then the road. Next they drew the road again, after which they also showed a character in the car, the protagonist walking out, and getting back to the car. The last one divided the fragment into nine scenes, showing the car (from the side) driving past an ocean in the back, then in front of mountains with two houses on the right side, and then zooming in on two people sitting in the car (seen from the front). Still with the car from the front, the character got out. Next, this character walked down the path (seeing the car from the side now), even further, then turned to go back, opened the car door, and then the view switched to show the hood of the car and open door, the character opening the door, and another character behind him holding up a stick.

Regarding spatial layout there were a few variations in this majority interpretation group. Three out of eight had the road diagonally across the page, from about top left towards bottom right (see Figure 3.14). The car was somewhere in the middle, with above the road either mountains (in two cases; including Figure 3.14) or trees. One of these three included the city behind the hills as well as a moon and stars. Three others then had the road more vertically aligned, so the car seemed to be going "up" rather than to the right of the page. These three all included an ocean in the top left corner, and two of them showed the car in the first scene from a bird's-eye view. One of them did not include a road when showing the protagonist walking, meaning they then drew the car from the side sitting above the horizon. This was also the case for the participant who included nine shifts whenever the car was drawn from the side.

The first subgroup, consisting of six drawings, drew a single scene with the protagonist standing outside the car. Five of them showed the car on the right side of the page, with the protagonist in front of or next to the car to the left (see Figure 3.15). The other had the car in the middle of the page with

Figure 3.15 First subgroup interpretation; notation reads "I perceive this scene in the dark, from a distance looking on" (arrows then indicate where the participant is looking: the background, the car, and the protagonist)

the protagonist on the right side, leaning on it. Three drawings included mountains in the background, mostly horizontally across the page. Two of these also included a moon, and one included light shading to possibly indicate a dark sky; another had dark shading, unmistakably meant to represent darkness. The other included a city along the horizon and described the dark in a note (see Figure 3.15). One of the participants that did not have mountains instead drew the ocean in the top left corner.

The second subgroup included three drawings that did not portray the protagonist outside the car. The first drawing here did not show the car immediately, but first only the road with hills in the back and a small path diverging from the road. The second scene then showed the car from the side. The other two drawings start roughly identical, with the car on the left side of the page on the road, with hills in the back. One of them included the ocean behind the hills as well (though one may want to consider it could also be fog), and included additional scenes beyond the aforementioned one (see Figure 3.16). Scene two illustrated the view from the driver, portraying only hands on the steering wheel and the road and trees through the window. The third scene was the car (seen from the side) driving towards a tree, with hatching all over it and a note that said "dark."

Figure 3.16 Second subgroup interpretation; notations read (from left to right) "1st" (these are references to which scene/viewpoint comes first), "2nd," "3rd," and "dark"

The final drawing based on this fragment was somewhat unclear. The first scene shows an ocean with hills behind it, and the second one shows the car from its side, and the protagonist beside it. The third scene, however, is not clear in its depiction. Perhaps the protagonist is standing beside hills or trees on the path, or is seen from within the car (with the objects then being the car's chairs). Then a stick is drawn moving through the air. Since it was somewhat ambiguous, this result was placed in its own subgroup. Overall, 15 drawings included the described hills (see Figures 3.14–3.16), eight indicated an ocean, and seven had some light lines across the page that could resemble fog (two of these were ambiguous but given the benefit of the doubt). Four participants then drew a city in the far background (see Figure 3.15), while one had houses up close, although the fragment specified there were actually "no houses." Seven had some indicated of the second character, "Mariott." One instance was female coded, namely, the character appeared to be wearing a skirt, even though the actual character is male (indicated in the fragment with the pronoun "he"). Then, 11 drawings included crosshatching, completely dark space, or a moon (with optional stars) to feature the dark setting described in the fragment (see Figure 3.15). Lastly, nine out of 20 participants drew the stick.

Regarding the viewpoint perceived by the participants, 13 drawings consistently presumed a perspective somewhat further away. Two drawings were consistent in adopting the narrator's viewpoint: one upheld this view from the narrator's eyes in the single scene they drew and the other upheld it for all scene shifts. The other five drawings switched between the two viewpoints. Four of them saw the car from far away first and adopted a perspective from the narrator's eyes, either when the protagonist was driving (two cases; Figures 3.14–3.16) or when he went outside of the car (two cases). The other drawing showed a view from the narrator's eyes while driving, and watched from further back as the protagonist was attacked.

3.2.2.7 Fragment 5: De Vergaderzaal *(Albert Alberts)*

BOX 3.11

Fragment 5

De secretaris stond bij het hoekraam van de vergaderzaal en keek naar buiten. Hij hoorde hoe achter zijn rug de concierge bezig was blocnotes en potloden over de tafel te verdelen.

Translation:

The secretary stood by the corner window of the conference hall and looked outside. He heard how behind him the janitor was distributing notepads and pencils around the table.

Here the majority interpretation was formed by six depictions that all indicated clear corners with either a window stretching across that corner (four cases; see Figure 3.17) or one window right next to it (two cases). Each time, the protagonist was in front of that window, with a table behind him. Figure 3.17 had the window and tables in the middle of the room. Two other corner windows were located on the right side of the page, which thus seemed to be the right side corner of the room, while the other half of this majority group had the windows on the left side of the page, thus seemingly placed in the left corner of the room. If the window was on the right side, the table was placed more to the left, and vice versa. For one other drawing besides Figure 3.17, the table was placed in the middle of the canvas. Within this majority interpretation, there were three round tables with chairs around them and pens and papers on top. There was

Figure 3.17 Majority interpretation

one depiction with a rectangular table and one depiction that included two rectangular tables, one big and one small. For the latter, the supposed secretary at the window had a desk for himself, with a chair and paper on top. This character was wearing clothes, namely a shirt and a skirt, and they had long hair. The supposed janitor character was wearing a shirt and pants and had short curly hair. This was the only participant to depict clothes, which likely were intended as typical outfits for females and males respectively. That would suggest the secretary was female and the janitor male in their visualization, although a "he" pronoun is used for the secretary in the fragment. Alternatively, they may have intended the secretary to be further from the window, and the janitor nearer to it, but this seems unlikely given the explicit positions in the text. The final drawing of this group is Figure 3.17, which showed small rectangular tables organized in a school setting, each with paper and pens on them. This was the only drawing to not include the janitor. As a last addition, two participants added a view seen from the window, namely a cityscape and trees, respectively (the latter exemplified in Figure 3.17).

The next two subgroups each consisted of two drawings. The first subgroup concerned those that did not show any corner, since these drawings did not indicate any walls. For one (see Figure 3.18), the window was on the left side of the canvas, with the protagonist (seen from the side) beside it,

Figure 3.18 First subgroup interpretation; notation reads "perspective from his eyes. Looks back to see"

and behind them on the right side of the page was a square table with pens and paper and the janitor on the far right. This participant was the second to include hair for any of the characters, namely, they included short curls for the secretary. For the other, the layout was flipped; the window was on the right side of the page, with the protagonist to the left of it, and behind him the janitor, distributing papers and pens on a round table in the left corner. Here too, one participant included a view seen through the window. It is unclear whether it is two trees, or one tree and a building.

The other subgroup was more divergent. These instances showed the scene from the outside, looking in through the window (see Figure 3.19). Thus, both looked upon the protagonist. One had a square table with papers and pens and the janitor on the right side of the protagonist, while the other showed only the janitor positioned towards the left side (Figure 3.19). The latter was the only depiction with no table.

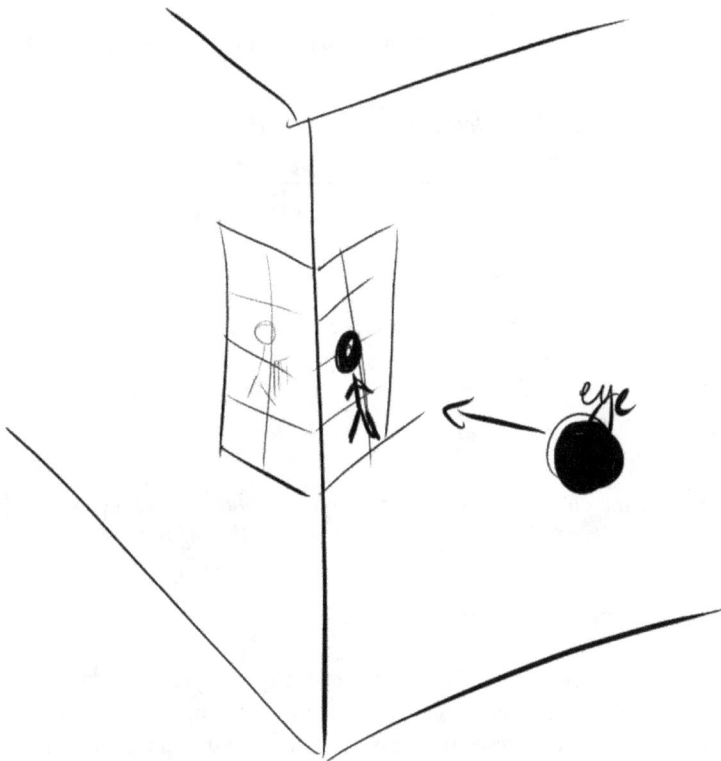

Figure 3.19 Second subgroup interpretation

Out of all ten drawings, six had a corner window that stretched across two walls (see Figures 3.17 and 3.19). Four of them had their reader viewpoint situated inside the room and two had it outside. Four drawings included a window that appeared as if on a single wall (see Figure 3.18). Nine out of ten included the janitor character, with nine instances of recognizable notepads and eight instances of pencils. Out of the nine tables depicted, five were rectangular and four were round. Most drawings had just a single table, but one drawing drew two (one near the secretary, one near the janitor) and another drew three small ones as if in a school setting (Figure 3.17). Six tables were accompanied by chairs.

Concerning the perceived viewpoint, eight out of ten participants experienced the scene from somewhat further away (see Figure 3.17). As described, two perspectives were from the outside (Figure 3.19), but most were in the room. Most were somewhat in the middle but some were more to the side, and one described that they were "standing at the door opposite the corner window." Two adopted the viewpoint of the narrator looking outside the window. One of them clarified that the narrator, shown to be looking outside the window, afterwards looked back at the janitor (Figure 3.18).

3.2.2.8 Fragment 5 Manipulated: De Vergaderzaal *(Albert Alberts)*

BOX 3.12

Fragment 5 Manipulated

Ik stond bij het hoekraam van de vergaderzaal en keek naar buiten. Ik hoorde hoe achter mijn rug de concierge bezig was blocnotes en potloden over de tafel te verdelen.

Translation:

I stood by the corner window of the conference hall and looked outside. I heard how behind me the janitor was distributing notepads and pencils around the table.

For this manipulated version as well, the majority interpretation contained six drawings with all clearly depicted corners, having windows either stretched across the two walls (five cases) or situated on a single wall (one case). All protagonists here were in front of the window, seen from behind, with a table behind them. Two of them were facing the right side of the canvas, while the other four were facing left. Two tables were round, one of them was small and square, and the other three were rectangular (see Figure 3.20). Four drawings did not include chairs, but all of them included the janitor and pens and/or papers. One room had as additional furniture a lamp and another included a whiteboard, a clock, and a coffee in the hand of the secretary (clarified through notes). One other participant also wrote down the secretary was holding a coffee, as well as wearing a "suit," looking out over an "industrialized area," while the janitor behind him was wearing "blue overalls." Regarding the view from the window, one other participant drew clouds, and another drew a tree.

The first subgroup then consisted of three participants that illustrated no clear corner (two cases; see Figure 3.20) or no window (one case). Regarding the former, one positioned the protagonist on the right side of the canvas, with presumably curtains in front of the window. The table was behind him on the left side of the canvas, with to the far left the janitor distributing paper and pens, who seemed to be wearing a hat. The table was

Figure 3.20 Majority interpretation; notations read "shifting perspective from 1. looking out the window to 2. seeing the whole room. Also many visual memories from high school"

round. The other positioned the protagonist directly in front of the window in the middle of the page, with the corner to the right somewhat further away (see Figure 3.20). The table was directly behind the protagonist; it was rectangular and surrounded by chairs. There were no paper or pens on top of it, and there was no janitor depicted. The final drawing in this subgroup then had no window, so the secretary seemed to be staring at the wall. Possibly, the wall is the window, but this remained ambiguous. The secretary was on the left side of the canvas, with a round table with paper on it behind him, and a janitor to the far right distributing pens.

The last drawing then resembled the more divergent subgroup of Fragment 5 in that the perspective looked over the shoulder of the protagonist into the room (Figure 3.21). One difference is that here, no window was visible, so the viewpoint was still located within the room rather than outside it. They included small, square desks similar to a school setting (although no chairs were drawn) and the janitor starting to place papers and pencils on them.

Out of the ten drawings, all but one included the janitor. This drawing (Figure 3.20) was also the only one not to depict notepads. Seven depictions included pencils. Half of the drawings showed a window stretching across two corners, while three had the window on a single one. Thus, two did

Figure 3.21 Subgroup interpretation; notation reads "over shoulder"

not indicate a window. Four out of ten tables were round, while two were square; the remainder were rectangular. Of the square tables, one depiction showed lots of them, again resembling a school setting. Four drawings then also included chairs.

Regarding the perceived viewpoint, six out of ten participants viewed this scene from somewhat further away. Most looked at the back of the protagonist from somewhere in the room, but one looked over the secretary's shoulder into the room. Three of them experienced shifts in scenes, namely first looking closely at the protagonist, and then zooming out to observe the room and/or the table specifically. Four participants adopted the narrator's perspective (at least partly). Half of them showed a single perspective, while the other two first looked out through the window through the protagonist's eyes, but then shifted to view the entire room (leaving the narrator's perspective).

3.2.2.9 Fragment 6: Karakter *(Ferdinand Bordewijk)*

BOX 3.13

Fragment 6

Aan het eind van de gang over zijn volle breedte liep een trap van zeven treden omhoog, zwaar beloperd, leidend naar een achttiende-eeuwse massieve deur. Die deur ging open. In het licht van een kroon met veel lampen, gesluierd door dichte sigarenrook, zag hij aan een lange groene tafel een aantal heren zitten, veel rode koppen. En aan het hoofdeinde zat een oud man met haar als van een grijze leeuw wiens manen slordig te berge zijn gerezen. Een opgewonden zware mannenstem zei driemaal achtereen, steeds de eerste lettergreep beklemtonend: "Absoluut, àbsoluut, àbsoluut."

Translation:

At the end of the hall, across its full width, a thickly carpeted, seven-stepped staircase ascended, leading to a massive eighteenth-century door. The door opened. In the light of a many crystalled chandelier, he saw, seated at a long, green table, a few red-faced gentlemen, veiled in thick cigar smoke. At the head of the table sat an old man with hair like that of a grey lion whose scruffy mane stands on end. An excited, deep voice said three times "Absolutely, absolutely, absolutely," each time emphasizing the first syllable.

Figure 3.22 Majority interpretation

Ten out of 20 drawings showed this fragment in at least two scenes, namely, the stairs and door (both seen from the front) and the room where people sat around the table. This formed the majority interpretation. Half of this group kept to viewing the table in the second room aligned vertically, meaning that the short side of it was turned towards the protagonist, with at the far end the old man with hair like that of a lion, as described in the fragment (see Figure 3.22). The other half saw the table on its long side, meaning the old man, recognizable again because of his hair, was seated either on the left end of the table (one case) or on the right (four cases). One of the tables was drawn from a bird's-eye view. Out of these ten depictions, just one seated a single person besides the old man at the table, while the rest all included multiple persons. In nine cases, this old man was indicated via noticeable hair, as outlined in the fragment (see Figure 3.22). Two participants zoomed in on this man, one of which drew him with a moustache and fancy suit, while the other showed him as a man, then as a lion, and then as a man again. Three out of ten times, the other persons in the room were shown smoking (see Figure 3.22). In one additional case, only the old man was smoking. Three times, there were also wavy lines to indicate smoke (see Figure 3.22), and two other times there was smoke but no cigars. Six drawings showed the chandelier inside the second room (see Figure 3.22). Regarding the hallway, one person indicated that there were "carpet holders" on the stairs. Another drew vertical lines along the stairs likely to show a carpet. One drawing included other doors along the hallway, besides the one at the end.

The first subgroup consisted of seven drawings showing just a single scene. Two of these were situated within the second room completely, showing no stairs. One showed the chandelier in the middle of the canvas, underneath the table with its short end towards the protagonist, who was standing in front of it. Along the sides were other people, and at the end, partly obscured by the chandelier, was the old man. The other participant showed just the table with people alongside it and with the old man at the end, holding a cigar. The chandelier was in the top right corner. The other five drawings did show the stairs. Three cases depicted part of the stairs and the open door through which one could see the table, either vertically (in two cases) or turned on its side (one case; see Figure 3.23). One of these participants showed the table and the stairs to be in the same room; the table was shown vertically (its short side towards the protagonist at the bottom of the page), with people alongside it and a chandelier hanging above. Behind the table, top middle of the canvas, was the big door, with in front of it a few stairs. The remaining two cases depicted the entire hallway, with the

Figure 3.23 First subgroup interpretation

full stairs in sight and at the stairs' end open doors that showed the table with people around it in the next room. Concerning additional notes, one participant wrote down that the old man wore "a grey suit." that the hallway had a "red carpet," and there were "paintings of important people," which were drawn, too. Moreover, this participant was the only one to place the chandelier in the hallway, rather than in the second room.

The last subgroup consisted of those depicting the staircase from its side (three cases). Two of these staircases went up diagonally, from bottom left to right (see Figure 3.24), while one was drawn in the reverse (this stairway had two twists, resembling a river almost). This latter person drew the room on the left side of the page, including the doors and behind it the table with people. Out of the two diagonal staircases, one had the room on the right of the canvas, similarly seen on its side, with people, smoke, and the chandelier inside. The other one (Figure 3.24) drew the second scene from a bird's-eye view, with the table aligned vertically, surrounded by people and smoke. At the bottom end of the table was a dot and arrow to show viewpoint, directed at a figure drawn with darker lines than the others, presumably the old man described in the fragment (as he is seated at the far end of the table).

Overall, two from the 20 depictions showed no explicit door. All but one drew the gentlemen described in the fragment (see Figures 3.22–3.24).

Figure 3.24 Second subgroup interpretation

That one participant included a single person besides the old man at the head of the table, instead of multiple people. Fifteen participants illustrated explicit hair for the man at the head of the table (Figures 3.22 and 3.23). In total, seven drawings included smoke in the room and three portrayed cigars. Two included the text spoken at the end of the fragment.

Regarding the perceived perspective that participants adopted, 13 participants experienced the scene from the narrator's eyes. For those depicting multiple scenes, seven showed the protagonist in one scene, but not the other. For example, four drawings showed the protagonist walking up the stairs but did not show them in the second room (and thus seemed to view the room from their eyes; see Figure 3.24) and two showed the reverse (no protagonist on the stairs, only in the room). The remaining four drawings specified no protagonist, and thus appeared to view everything from their perspective (see Figure 3.22). One participant confirmed this by including the note: "perspective of the figure." Someone depicting a single scene included a similar note, reading "from eyes of narrator." Concerning those that viewed the scene from somewhat further away, these were situated behind the narrator. One of them clarified that they had "no body" and were "more like floating/a ghost."

3.2.2.10 Fragment 7: Nooit Meer Slapen *(Willem Frederik Hermans)*

BOX 3.14

Fragment 7

Midden op het plein staat een monument van blauw brons, een man in poolkleding op een vierkante sokkel. Hiervandaan zie ik hem op z'n rug. Wie is hij? Ik loop erheen en lees de naam die op de sokkel staat: ROALD AMUNDSEN.

Translation:

In the middle of the square there stands a monument of blue copper; it's of a man in arctic clothing on a square pedestal. From where I stand, I am looking at his back. Who is he? I walk towards it and read the name that is written on the pedestal: ROALD AMUNDSEN.

Six out of ten drawings form the majority interpretation since all show the statue from either its front or back with the protagonist (or the reader

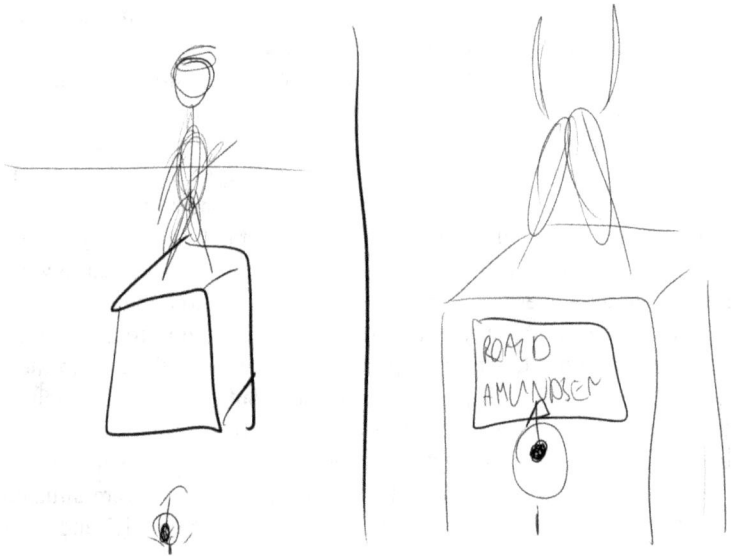

Figure 3.25 Majority interpretation; plaque reads "Roald Amundsen"

viewpoint) in front of it. Four of these had an additional scene to zoom in on the plaque (see Figure 3.25). One of them drew the plaque with "Roald Amundsen" on it next to the first scene. Two others zoomed in more clearly, namely, one redrew the top part of the statue and the protagonist's head partly in front of the plaque (Figure 3.25). The other drew the statue from the front and indicated that they first looked at the statue and his pedestal, then at the statue more closely, and finally at the plaque below his feet. The fourth drawing used four scenes. The first depicted the statue from far away (with a note: *"far away, see the square and city"*) and the second zoomed in on the statue from the narrator's eyes (showing the statue's feet and the back of the protagonist's head; a note clarified *"from his p.o.v."*). The third then zoomed out again to watch him walk around the statue (stating *"far away during walking"*), and the last scene adopts the narrator's perspective again to read the plaque (shown from up close with only the feet of the statue visible as well; a note reads *"see what he is reading up close"*). The two other depictions in this majority interpretation group walk around the statue. One showed the statue from the back and then from the front, including the name. The other one first shows the statue from its front, shown by the face drawn on top of the statue's head. Their next scene then shows the statue from the back, with a dotted line to resemble the protagonist walking around it to read the text. This is then the only participant to not include a plaque including text or scribbles resembling text. From the total six drawings, half of them include clear clothing for the statue. Two also show buildings in the background.

The first subgroup then has two drawings drawn from a remarkably high perspective. One is a bird's-eye view, showing a diamond shape that represents the square, with within it another diamond shape to denote the pedestal. Within that shape is a circle that should portray the statue. The protagonist then is on the left side of the canvas. The other drawing in this subgroup is also from high up, but shows the pedestal and statue from the side, as well as some buildings in the background (Figure 3.26). Similarly, they show just the one scene of the protagonist staring at the statue. This drawing was also the only one to include other people on the square, namely three.

The next subgroup drawing then depicted the statue from its side in the middle of the canvas, with the protagonist to the left. The plaque was drawn as a satellite bubble above the pedestal, since there was no room to write the text on that side. Two notes clarified that the statue was wearing an "*arctic hat*" and "*arctic clothing*," which were also drawn.

The final drawing, and subgroup, then showed only the feet of the statue and the text below his feet. With a note, this participant clarified that they "looked upwards from the feet to the whole statue." This plaque was the only one to include a date, namely 1950–1970.

Figure 3.26 First subgroup interpretation

Figure 3.27 Second subgroup interpretation; notations read (from left to right) *"views," "Roald Amundsen," "artic hat," and "artic clothing"* (in Dutch)

Overall, all ten drawings depicted a square pedestal as described in the fragment. Six included a readable name on there too, while one had "Roald" clearly and then portrayed the surname through scribbles. Three statues were wearing obvious arctic clothing, sometimes indicated as such with a note (see Figure 3.27). Two drawings added buildings in the background and one of those also included additional people on the square (Figure 3.26).

Concerning the perceived viewpoint, eight out of ten participants adopted the narrator's perspective (see Figures 3.25 and 3.26). Two of these did not even draw narrators, which is why they are presumed to view this scene from their eyes. One indicated a figure labelled "me," which could be ambiguous (whether the figure is just the reader or a merge between reader and narrator). However, this participant used this label consistently throughout their drawings, so we can confidently assume that this portrays a merge of reader and narrator, as it did for their other drawings. The rest clearly indicated that they adopted the narrator's viewpoint via arrows originating from the protagonist's head or notes ("from protag's eyes" or "from the eyes of the narrator"). One participant experienced shifts between viewpoints; this participant had included the four scenes. In the first and third scene, they included notes reading "far away, see whole square + city" and "far away during walking," respectively. Similarly, when depicting the scenes with the statue's feet they mentioned "from his [the narrator's] p.o.v." and "see what he reads up close." The final participant, watching this scene from somewhat further away, drew a reader figure (recognized as such because of a viewpoint symbol above their head) behind the protagonist, so they were watching the protagonist from behind (Figure 3.27).

3.2.2.11 Fragment 7 Manipulated: Nooit Meer Slapen (Willem Frederik Hermans)

BOX 3.15

Fragment 7 Manipulated

Midden op het plein staat een monument van blauw brons, een man in poolkleding op een vierkante sokkel. Hiervandaan ziet hij hem op z'n rug. Wie is hij? Alfred loopt erheen en leest de naam die op de sokkel staat: ROALD AMUNDSEN.

Translation:

In the middle of the square there stands a monument of blue copper; it's of a man in arctic clothing on a square pedestal. From where he stands, he is looking at his back. Who is he? Alfred walks towards it and reads the name that is written on the pedestal: ROALD AMUNDSEN.

Nine out of ten drawings show the statue from either its front or its back with the protagonist (or the reader viewpoint) in front of it similar to the previous majority interpretation. Similarly, distinctions can be made between those experiencing shifts in scenes and those depicting just one. For the four drawings that included shifts (see Figure 3.28), there were either two, three, four, or five scenes. With two scenes, the first depicted the statue seemingly from its rear, in arctic clothing, with the protagonist (labelled "Alfred") in front of it looking at it. In the background were buildings that were labelled "houses, shops, etc." The second scene then showed the protagonist from the side, looking at the words "Roald Amundsen" below the statue's feet, now seen mostly from the side. The three-shift drawing had one scene on the page, but notations for three varying perspectives. The scene itself was the statue on a pedestal in the middle of the canvas, with houses in the

Figure 3.28 Majority interpretation; notations read (from left to right) "front,"
"following Alfred walking," "Roald Amundsen," and "back"

background. The protagonist was towards the right and drawn smaller, so
they were seemingly behind the statue. The participant first looked at the
statue, then at either his face or his back (this remains ambiguous, as the
arrow is pointed towards the face, but could also refer to the back of the
head), and, lastly, the scene from further away. The four-scene drawing
(Figure 3.28) starts with the statue from the "front" (as indicated by a note),
with two buildings in the back. The second then clarified we were watching the "back" of the statue and portrays the protagonist standing near the
bottom of the page (so "in front of" the back of the statue). The third scene
then showed the legs of the statue, with the protagonist in front of it, and
a note that said, "following Alfred walking." Lastly, the plaque with the
text was shown up close. For the final five-shift drawing, there were notes
specifying each viewpoint as well. Here, the participant drew the statue
once on the page (wearing a cap and holding, presumably, a fishing rod),
including a plaque with "R A" on it, but drew the protagonist twice to show
various scenes. One time the protagonist was towards the left, in front of
the statue and seen from behind, and once towards the right, behind the
statue and seen from the front. The first scene had to show the "*surroundings, man* [the protagonist], *statue from the front*." It is ambiguous whether

the participant here views the protagonist from behind or from the front, but we presume the latter because of the next scene. The second scene included the protagonist on the right side (behind the statue and seen from the front) as the viewpoint number was placed right next to him, and the note read "*man, then the statue from behind.*" The protagonist on the right was looking at the statue's back, indicated by an arrow originating from the protagonist's eyes. The third scene was described as "*man walks,*" with an arrow starting at the protagonist on the right and moving towards the protagonist on the left, suggesting that you follow the path from the protagonist walking around the pedestal towards the statue's front. The fourth scene then depicted the "*back of [the] man,*" which referred to the protagonist on the left of the page, now in front of the statue. The final scene was indicated by a circle drawn around the plaque, and that they viewed the "*name [of the] statue.*"

Regarding the six drawings of the majority interpretation that did not experience shifts in scenes, half of them placed the statue in the middle of the canvas, and two of them added houses in the background. Concerning the other half of single-scene depictions, these drawings showed the statue at a slight angle. Two of them let it face the left, while the other had the

Figure 3.29 Subgroup interpretation

statue face more to the right. One included crosshatching to possibly depict cobblestones. Two of these three showed clear artic clothing as well.

One drawing formed a subgroup, as they placed the protagonist clearly to the side of the statue rather than somewhere in front of it, and who were thus unable to read the text on the plaque (Figure 3.29). The statue, wearing a "snowsuit" (labelled as such), was seen from the front, with its name on the plaque below its feet. A note specified that the character to the right of the pedestal was the "main character." Furthermore, there were elaborate houses in the back, specified as *half-timbered houses.* The square was also laid with "cobblestones."

Out of all ten drawings, again each one depicted the statue on a square pedestal, as described in the fragment. Six gave the statue recognizable artic clothing (see Figure 3.29), and five had the figure's name on the plaque in a readable manner. One other just wrote the initials (R.A.) and one other had scribbles instead. Lastly, five depicted buildings in the background (see Figure 3.29).

For the perceived viewpoint, six participants viewed the scene from somewhat further away, watching the statue's front or back with usually the protagonist (or just a viewpoint) in front of it (see Figure 3.29). One time, the narrator was next to the statue, with the viewpoint at the bottom of the page, viewing the scene the way it was drawn. Half of the participants with this perspective followed Alfred around the statue, and thus perceived the scene from multiple angles. Two of them zoomed in on the name on the plaque for their final viewpoint. One of them drew this plaque up close with no narrator near, suggesting that here, they did momentarily share their perspective while reading the text (Figure 3.28). Four participants clearly shared the narrator's perspective. Two drew clear arrows originating from the narrator's eyes to indicate viewpoint and two others drew no narrator, but one of them clarified through a note that the scene was perceived "from Alfred's eyes."

3.2.2.12 Fragment 8: Lijmen *(Willem Elsschot)*

BOX 3.16

Fragment 8

Ik had den man, die één tafel verder tegenover mij zat, reeds een paar keer aangekeken, want hij riep herinneringen in mij wakker, al wist ik zeker dat ik nooit met zoo iemand had omgegaan. Hij zag er voorspoedig en burgerlijk uit, als een man van zaken, en toch deed hij mij denken aan Vlaamscheleeuwen vlaggen en Guldensporenslagen, aan jongens met baarden en vilthoeden. In zijn knoopsgat zat een decoratie en naast hem, op de tafel, lagen een paar keurige handschoenen. Neen, ik had nooit omgang gehad met menschen van dat soort en toch kon ik mijn blik niet van hem afwenden. Waar, waar, waar?

Translation:

I had looked at that man, who was sitting at the next table opposite me, a few times already, because he roused memories in me, even though I knew for sure I had never met the likes of him. He looked successful and bourgeois, like a man of enterprise, and yet he reminded me of the Flemish lion flag and The Battle of the Golden Spurs, of young men with beards and felt hats. In his buttonhole there was a decoration and next to him, on the table, lay a pair of neat gloves. No, I had never associated with people of that sort, but, still, I could not avert my gaze from him. Where, where, where?

Figure 3.30 Majority interpretation; notations read (from left to right) "*where, where, where?*" "*decoration in buttonhole*," and "*gloves*" (in Dutch)

The majority interpretation is formed by 14 drawings that show the protagonist in the foreground relative to the table with the described man, which is placed further back (see Figure 3.30). All but one look (mostly) at the protagonist's back. The one divergent drawing shows the protagonist seated with his back to the described man, and the viewpoint originating from the chair opposite the protagonist. Thus, in this case, the protagonist would be turning around to look at the man. Regarding placement on the page, eight out of 14 had the protagonist sitting at their own table around the middle or bottom left of the canvas, and the table with the man being described more towards the right side (see Figure 3.30). Three drawings had the protagonist more towards bottom right, so the described man was towards the left of the canvas. Three others then had the protagonist and the described man aligned, so both were placed roughly in the middle of the scene. Out of these 14 depictions, nine drew the protagonist seated at a table as well (see Figure 3.30). The remaining five were split between drawing only the table and not the protagonist, so as if adopting the protagonist's viewpoint (three cases), and drawing only the protagonist' upper body but no table (two cases). Regarding the tables, five depictions included multiple tables in addition to the one the described man was sitting at and (optionally) the protagonist's table (see Figure 3.30). Mostly, these additional tables were empty (Figure 3.30), but in two cases there were other people sitting at them. This elicited a restaurant setting, which two participants specified through notes as well ("this happens in a fancy restaurant, they're wearing smart clothes" and "picture a restaurant"). One other clarified it was a bar, by drawing something resembling it in the background and labelling it "bar." This was also one of the two drawings to have round tables, instead of small square ones like the rest. Aligning with the idea of the bar was their note specifying that the protagonist was holding "*beer.*" Other drawings implied a restaurant setting by including plates and/or glasses (in four cases; see Figure 3.30) or just glasses/mugs (in three other cases). Three added candles; the drawing noting it was a "fancy restaurant" even specified it was a "candelabra." This was also the only one to include a "landscape painting" (labelled as such) and companions for both the protagonist and the "guy he keeps looking at." For the former, the companion had long hair and a bow on top of their head, implying most likely that this is a woman, and, for the latter, a note indicated that "his companion has just gone to the toilet." Besides the plates and/or glasses, 12 out of 14 depictions showed the gloves on the table (see Figure 3.30). Moreover, nine depictions included clothes resembling a suit or similarly fancy wear, or a hat. Four specifically drew or labelled the decoration mentioned in the fragment (Figure 3.30). Within this majority interpretation, two depictions included multiple scenes. One first showed the table with the described man sitting at the far end, including a chair opposite him. Then the drawing just zoomed in on the man sitting at the table, so only half of the table remained visible; as they said, they "zoom in [for] more details," and likewise now drew gloves on the table and the man in a suit with a beard. The other drawing first showed the protagonist at his own table watching the man at his, before similarly zooming in on that man, now in a suit (indicated with the note "fancy shirt 'n stuff"). Then this participant illustrated a lion, people with weapons in hand (labelled "war, *battle of the Golden Spurs*") and a man with a beard seen from the side, wearing a hat, in three separate scenes that were seen "not really [from] a viewpoint, just frontal like this." Next, they drew the man being described again, focusing on the decoration first and then the gloves on the table. Last, they redrew the man in his suit and with the gloves near, and specified they were "looking at [the] scene from afar."

The remaining six drawings constituted the subgroup, since all drew the two tables from the side. Two of them had the described man sitting at the table on the left, while the other four drawings seated him at the table on the right (see Figure 3.31). The protagonist then sat at the table on the opposite side. Admittedly, two drawings were somewhat ambiguous. One showed two people at the table opposite the described man's table. One sat seemingly with their back to that man and the other character was where

Figure 3.31 Subgroup interpretation first example; notations read (from left to right) "*see the scene from far*," "*where*," and "*zoom in on buttonhole*" (in Dutch)

the reader's viewpoint originated (labelled as "eye" with an arrow originating from that head). Either this was the protagonist and the reader adopted their viewpoint, or the other character at the table was the protagonist that the reader looked upon. The other ambiguous drawing drew two tables, with one character sitting on the left side, and the other character at the other table sitting on the right side. The first viewpoint then looked at the character on the left, and the second viewpoint looked at both characters. The third then zoomed in, and resembled the right character's posture (typical stick figure with arms up and legs spread), but with clothes on. Either the character at the table on the right is the protagonist, looking at the man being described sitting at the left table, or this character is the described man as well, shown now sitting at a different side of the table, but with the third scene zooming in on him specifically.

Out of the six depictions in the subgroup, half of the tables were round (see Figure 3.31), while the other half were drawn as either square or rectangular. In this subgroup, only one drawing included a glass/mug and just one a plate. Two participants included more tables than just those of the main characters and both specified it was a "restaurant" or "restaurant setting." One of them also portrayed other people sitting at those tables, as

Figure 3.32 Subgroup interpretation second example; notations read (from top to bottom) "what protag saw" and "what he thought he saw"

well as a window, and notes to describe the clothing of the main characters. The protagonist *"didn't wear a suit"* and the other man had *"neat hair"* and *"wears a suit with a decoration."* Of the remaining five, two included hats for the man being described (see Figure 3.31), while two others included clothes (significant mostly because the protagonist did not have any). The last participant diverged slightly (see Figure 3.32). They drew the protagonist at a table on the left side, looking at a man at a table in the top right corner, with in front of him a plate and two mittens. A note read "what the protag saw." Below that in the bottom right corner was a cloud encompassing a man with beard and fancy hat, sitting at a table with gloves in front of him. Here a note stated: "what he thought he saw." Thus, this participant imagined the protagonist staring at a normal man, but visualizing him as someone else, wearing fancy clothes. Similar to this, there were two other drawings portraying shifts. One just zoomed in on the decoration in a separate scene, writing *"zoom in on buttonhole"* (Figure 3.31). The other viewed the man being described first, then zoomed out to also show the protagonist sitting at the opposite table. Third, they viewed the man separately from his table, after which they drew the described flag, three circles that possibly depict (gold) coins, two men with beards and hats, something that possibly resembles a flower sticking out from a jacket, and, lastly, the gloves. It is important to note that not all of these separate illustrations could be identified clearly, but this interpretation is deemed most probable due to the descriptions in the fragment.

Overall, two participants across these two groups included the protagonist's thoughts (*"Where, where, where?"*). One of them wrote those three words in a thought bubble, while the other included just one *"where"* next to the protagonist's head (Figure 3.31). Out of the total 20 drawings, four specified the restaurant setting through notes, and one clarified it as a bar. Eight participants included plates and/or glasses and seven showed multiple tables in the room, three of which placed other people at them. Fifteen participants included a suit (or otherwise nice clothes) or hat for the described man and 18 drew his gloves near him. Last, seven indicated a decoration as described in the fragment.

Regarding the perceived viewpoint of the readers, 11 out of 20 participants adopted the narrator's point of view (see Figure 3.30). Four were very explicit in portraying this, since three drew no narrator but just the view from the table is if seated at it. Meaning, in two cases one saw only the far edge of the table with plates or a candle in front of them, and one showed a hand holding a mug. They also wrote "from the eyes of the narrator." The other case showed no table's edge, but did write "perspective of the I" to clarify. The last of these four coloured in the protagonist's head (the character seated at the table opposite of the described man's table) and wrote "me" above it, which suggests the reader here merges with the narrator. Six out of 20 then viewed the scene from further away. One of them first watched the back of the narrator and then the "*other man from far away.*" Three drawings with the viewpoint from further away also depict the tables from the side (see Figures 3.31 and 3.32). In total, six depictions had portrayed the tables from the side. One of these switched between viewpoints, first looking upon both tables, but then adopting the viewpoint from the narrator, looking upon the man being described. The final two drawings that showed the tables from the side had an ambiguous viewpoint, so it was difficult to tell if they adopted the narrator's perspective. As described in the subgroup analysis above, it was not clear in these drawings which character was the narrator. One depiction might have the reader taking the narrator's view, but could also be looking at the narrator, with the man being described then visible behind him. The other depiction either has two separate tables with the man being described and the protagonist, respectively, or has the same table twice and the man being described switched to the other side.

3.3 Interim Discussion

In addition to the results outlined in detail above, participants also filled in a post-experiment questionnaire. The first four questions asked whether they read any of the books (we listed the titles and authors), and, if so, in which language, how long ago, and if they remembered having read the selected fragment during the experiment. Four out of 20 participants indicated that they read one or more of the books. One read *Jane Eyre* and a part of *Nooit Meer Slapen*, in English and Dutch, respectively, seven and five years ago. They remembered only the fragment from *Jane Eyre* during the experiment, not the other one. The second participant just read *Jane Eyre*, in English, one year ago (twice), but did not remember the fragment during the experiment. The third read *Lijmen* in Dutch while in high school, which was seven years ago, but similarly did not recall this. The fourth read *The Garden of Eden* and *De Vergaderzaal*, in English and Dutch, respectively, four years ago. Like the other three, they did not remember the fragment during the experiment.

The next part of the questionnaire asked if any of the fragments themselves were known to them in another way prior to the experiment. Six people responded to this question (with something other than 'no' or 'n.a.'). One person commented that the writing style of the first fragment (*Garden of Eden*, Ernest Hemingway) reminded them of *East of Eden* and *Anna Karenina*, because the descriptive writing style was similar. The participant who read *Jane Eyre* and *Nooit Meer Slapen* (partly) mentioned here that, besides *Jane Eyre*, other fragments also felt slightly familiar, but they could not remember. A third participant answered to this question that they read parts of Bordewijk and Elsschot in secondary school but was unsure if it pertained to these fragments specifically. They did recognize the writing style. Another answer was that "one thing I found difficult is showing where exactly I was looking from, it ends up quite flat on the screen, it's hard to represent it spatially." Likewise, a fourth person said, "Honestly, I did not understand some of the words." Finally, one participant thought that the Bordewijk fragment felt familiar.

The final part of the questionnaire inquired after technical difficulties or other distractions, and whether the participants experienced dyslexia or similar reading disabilities. Just two had dyslexia (one of whom said it was "slight") and one was "just a naturally slow reader." Eight participants noted some kind of difficulty. Two mentioned how more movement in the scene made it more difficult (one specified "made drawing it more difficult"). One struggled with some of the English, as it was not their native language, and they felt some context was missing. Similarly, someone else struggled with depicting their mind's eye in drawing and that "deciding what to leave out is hard." Related to drawing was one comment that said, "not a great drawer," although this of course does not mean they thought it difficult to depict what they saw. The sixth person found the longer fragments harder, since forming an image and processing all information at the same time took them longer. Yet another mentioned Dutch was more boring, but recognized that that might be a personal opinion. The last said they were confused by the button on the pen they were using. When pressed, it functions as an eyedropper tool, which they perhaps accidentally activated during the experiment.

Overall, only one participant clearly remembered having read a fragment once before. For some, the writing style felt familiar, but hardly anyone knew the fragments beforehand or recognized them during the experiment. Hence, we can safely conclude that the fragments were unfamiliar to most, and that participants were not guided by prior knowledge of the storyline or the story world environment. Of the eight participants who provided comments relating to difficulties, five were actually pertaining to visualizing scenes in their mind or putting them on paper (the core task of this experiment).

We now turn towards the drawings again, providing a broader overview of our results from the previous section with the theory of Chapter 2 in mind. A detailed discussion of our results and their implications follows in Chapter 5. Some of the participants' comments resonate nicely with our findings, as will be outlined in the coming sections. To shape our further discussion, Table 3.1 summarizes the characteristics of the results per fragment.

Table 3.1 An overview per fragment, with manipulations as a separate version, of the point of view in the text, the perceived point of view, the number of groupings, a description of them, and the proportion of shifts (relative to the total amount of drawings)

Fragment number and name	Point of view in the text	Proportion reader point of view	Amount of interpretation groupings	Short description of interpretation groupings	Proportion of drawings including shifts
1 – Garden of Eden, Ernest Hemingway	Third person	Further away: 9/10, Narrator's eyes: 1/10	3	Majority group: protagonist in room near window, view possible. First subgroup: including inside and outside scene. Second subgroup: protagonist in room, view impossible	0/10
1 Manipulated – Garden of Eden, Ernest Hemingway	First person	Further away: 6/10, Narrator's eyes: 4/10	3	Majority group: protagonist in room near window, view possible. First subgroup: protagonist in room, view impossible. Second subgroup: including inside and outside scene	2/10
2 – The Crow Road, Iain Banks	Third person	Further away: 14/20, Narrator's eyes: 6/20	3	Majority group: protagonist in front of wall, look upon the back (varying backgrounds). First subgroup: showed protagonist and bridge from the side. Second subgroup: look at protagonist from the front	7/20
3 – Jane Eyre, Charlotte Brontë	First person	Further away: 6/10, Narrator's eyes: 4/10	2	Majority group: protagonist reading near the window, bookcase in the same room. Subgroup: ambiguous whether bookcase and window were in the same room	4/10

3 Manipulated – *Jane Eyre*, Charlotte Brontë	Third person	**Further away: 7/10** Narrator's eyes: 3/10	4	Majority group: protagonist reading near the window, bookcase in the same room First subgroup: ambiguous whether bookcase and window were in the same room Second subgroup: bookcase and window in separate spaces Third subgroup: no window	7/10
4 – *Farewell, My Lovely*, Raymond Chandler	First person	**Further away: 13/20** Narrator's eyes: 7/20	4	Majority group: protagonist walks around car in multiple scenes First subgroup: single scene with protagonist outside car Second subgroup: protagonist remains in car Third subgroup: ambiguous (protagonist walks outside, third scene unclear)	13/20
5 – *De Vergaderzaal*, Albert Alberts	Third person	**Further away: 8/10** Narrator's eyes: 2/10	3	Majority group: clear corner with protagonist in front of window First subgroup: no corner/walls Second subgroup: look through the window inside the room	2/10
5 – Manipulated – *De Vergaderzaal*, Albert Alberts	First person	**Further away: 6/10** Narrator's eyes: 4/10	3	Majority group: clear corner with protagonist in front of window First subgroup: no corner or window Second subgroup: look over protagonist's shoulder into the room	5/10

(Continued)

Table 3.1 (Continued)

Fragment number and name	Point of view in the text	Proportion reader point of view	Amount of interpretation groupings	Short description of interpretation groupings	Proportion of drawings including shifts
6 – Karakter, Ferdinand Bordewijk	Third person	Further away: 7/20 **Narrator's eyes: 13/20**	3	Majority group: multiple scenes showing the staircase/door from the front and the room with people First subgroup: single scenes of just the room with people (with and without part of the stairs) Second subgroup: showed the staircase from the side with the room either attached or from bird's-eye view	12/20
7 – Nooit Meer Slapen, Willem Frederik Hermans	First person	Further away: 2/10 **Narrator's eyes: 8/10**	4	Majority group: look at statue's front/back with protagonist/reader viewpoint in front of it First subgroup: single scene from very high up Second subgroup: statue seen from the side with protagonist next to it Third subgroup: shows only the statue's feet	5/10
7 – Manipulated – Nooit Meer Slapen, Willem Frederik Hermans	Third person	**Further away: 6/10** Narrator's eyes: 4/10	2	Majority group: look at statue's front/back with protagonist/reader viewpoint in front of it Subgroup: statue seen from the front with protagonist next to it	4/10
8 – Lijmen, Willem Elsschot	First person	Further away: 9/20 **Narrator's eyes: 11/20**	2	Majority group: protagonist in foreground with described man at a table further back Subgroup: showed the tables with protagonist and described man from the side	8/20

3.3.1 Point of View and Language

Overall, the analyses of the results provide an extensive range of variety, but remarkable similarity as well. Regarding the differences within each fragment, there were two to four subgroups for most. Some variations between subgroups were quite divergent, such as when the participants imagined themselves as being outside the room looking in through the window rather than being present in the room itself as most did. Alternatively, some followed the events described in the fragments rather closely in their imagination via creating new visions for new actions, while others represented a single scene. Other variations were less distinct, such as when it concerned the layout of the tables (aligned vertically or horizontally), whether an outside view was possible, or whether a bookcase and window were within the same space or separated. Some adopted a divergent manner of drawing the scene, such as using bird's-eye views even when they visualized it from the narrator's perspective. Most likely, this way of drawing is simply less complex than using perspective drawing. Some still used that complex perspective technique, depicting only the arms or legs of a narrator when they shared their perspective.

Regarding similarity across fragments, most fragments that had original and manipulated versions could be divided into mostly the same subgroups and also shared largely the same perspective from which that scene was viewed. Fragment 1 and 1M (*The Garden of Eden*, Ernest Hemingway) evoked highly similar groupings, with the majority interpretation placing the protagonist in a room near a window, so the protagonist was able to look outside. The minority groupings then pictured the outside view as inaccessible and depicted both the outside and inside simultaneously. One noticeable difference was that Fragment 1M, in a first-person perspective, had three window seats, whereas the 1M (third-person perspective) had none. Perhaps the use of "I" as a pronoun drew readers closer to the window. It did appear to help to share the narrator's viewpoint, which was done so four times for the first-person text, opposed to just once for the third-person one. Fragment 3 and 3M (*Jane Eyre*, Charlotte Brontë) shared the first two groups, namely, the majority interpretation visualizing the bookcase and window in the same space, and the first subgroup that was ambiguous in that regard. Only Fragment 3M then yielded two more subgroups: one where those aspects were clearly in separate spaces and one where there was no window. Both of them also had a slight majority of participants indicate that they perceived this scene from further away, despite the difference of the third-person and first-person perspective. Fragment 5 and 5M (*De Vergaderzaal*, Albert Alberts) had similar groupings throughout. The majority interpretation had a clear corner and window, with the protagonist in front of the window. The first subgroup then had no clear corner and either no walls or no window. The second subgroup looked at the front of the protagonist rather than his back, looking either through the window from outside the room or over the protagonist's shoulder from within the room. Again, most participants pictured the scenes from further away, irrespective of the perspective the scene was written in. Admittedly, the proportion decreased slightly for the first-person perspective (six out of ten, opposed to eight out of ten for the third-person text). Lastly then, Fragment 7 and 7M (*Nooit Meer Slapen*, Willem Frederik Hermans) shared the majority interpretation that placed the protagonist in front of the statue. One other subgroup aligned largely, with Fragment 7 having a drawing depicting the statue from its side and the protagonist next to it (looking at the statue's front), while Fragment 7M had a drawing showing the statue from the front, but the protagonist next to it unable to read the text on the plaque. Fragment 7 then had two more subgroups, one that assumed a high perspective on the scene and another that showed only the statue's feet. Regarding perceived perspective, there was a difference between the fragment written in third person and first person: the former yielded a majority for viewpoints from further away, while the latter elicited most participants to adopt the narrator's view. All in all, that there are similar groupings throughout is no more than sensible since both fragments describe the same elements within the same space. The essential difference was the viewpoint from which readers would perceive the scene. Apparently, neither perspective could persuade all readers to adopt a consistent stance; both third-person and first-person language led to a variety of interpretations. Most of these were set on viewing the scene from further away, no matter the perspective employed.

Overall, when also including the fragments that had just a singular version, the reader still witnessed most scenes from somewhat further away. One possible explanation may be the length of the fragments, as 2–12 lines could be deemed too short to identify with the narrator enough to adopt their perspective completely. As a counterpoint, even in the short fragments, some participants indicated shifts, sometimes switching between a viewpoint from further away to suddenly adopting the narrator's perspective. Furthermore, some persisted in viewing the scene through the narrator's eyes throughout, or they experienced just one scene that way. Thus, length is not solely responsible for allowing readers to immerse themselves. The implications of the language, even in short pieces, could already encourage readers to visualize themselves in the protagonist's place. This then apparently relies on factors more personal to the reader rather than something inherent in the manner of writing. Furthermore, even if it was a minority for most first-person fragments, there were always participants able to take the narrator's perspective. In fact, not one fragment had results that were unanimous. Each fragment elicited viewpoints from further away as well as viewpoints identical to the narrator across participants. Therefore, this further suggests that language alone does not persuade readers of a singular interpretation. Moreover, across fragments, two participants imagined every text from a perspective further away and two imagined scenes solely from the narrator's perspective. For these four participants, the language of the text did not affect their imagined viewpoints.

In addition to length, context should be taken into account. In this experiment, we presented the fragments completely free of any title, author, or synopsis, to direct the participants' attention solely to the text at hand. Such decontextualized extracts might be harder to interpret as they lack an introduction to build on. All characters and environments were new to readers and potentially feel foreign as a result. The descriptions within the fragments still made sense, but they could be more meaningful when supported by background knowledge of the narrator's previous location or relation to other characters. For example, if the breakfast room, from Fragment 3, had been described previously, it may have elicited more elaborate depictions when reading the current fragment as it is. Even if the fragment participants were given to read then does not describe it, previous (memorized) descriptions could lead participants to build upon that knowledge and include that room even more often by association. Likewise, Fragment 1 currently does not state the furniture the protagonist is sitting on, causing participants to image beds, couches, chairs, and window seats. Background knowledge of whether this space is a bedroom or not would maybe eradicate these variations. As a last, more subtle example, some participants depicted some stereotypical gender presentations, such as skirts, bows, and varying lengths of hair. Awareness of characters' gender, perhaps previously indicated with pronouns, may either encourage more of such presentations or correct mistaken ones (e.g. one participant drew "Marriot" with a dress, implying a feminine gender, despite the pronoun "he").

Lastly, regarding the choice of language, the 12 different fragments presented were divided into six English ones and six Dutch ones. There is minimal indication that this affected the imagined perspective of readers. One observation is that for the Dutch texts, three out of six fragments were predominantly perceived from the eyes of the narrator, while this was zero for the English texts. Two out of these three cases also concerned fragments written in first-person perspectives, which may hypothetically encourage sharing the protagonist's viewpoint. A preliminary idea might be that adopting the narrator's perspective could be more accessible in one's mother tongue. Nevertheless, it is necessary to also consider the order of presentation, which may just as well have been influential. Namely, the Dutch fragments were presented last. Possibly, readers became more familiar with the task of first reading and then drawing their mind's eye's representation, which may have then facilitated immersion. As our results base themselves on a relatively small sample, we advise caution with interpreting this data, but encourage further developments of our observations so far.

3.3.2 Deixis and Shifts

As outlined in Chapter 2, we consider deixis to be a possible impactful factor too with regards to the reader's imagined viewpoints. While spatial deictics are argued to guide the reader through a landscape or environment, this could have the side effect of distancing the reader from the narrator. As Kuzmičová (2014) points out, extracts with plentiful spatial indicators may create the impression of neither an enactment-image (visualizing the scene and adopting the narrator's (sensorimotor) experience) nor a description-image (visualizing the scene from outside the story world). These two terms loosely align with our classification of adopting the narrator's perspective (sharing their vision) and viewing the scene from further away (at times indicated by participants by drawing a third "spectator" character which the reader then inhabits, rather than a character from the story). Additionally, Kuzmičová offers a reiteration of the aforementioned speculation that readers may start out extrinsically by default. Recall also the related notion of Stockwell (2002; see Section 2.2), who described that the directionality of deixis may either "push" (prompt the reader to track the perception of a narrator) or "pop" (return the reader to their own world, as it were). In the following quote Kuzmičová discusses an extended version of the same Hemingway fragment also used in this research; David is the protagonist.

> For some, the in-between experience may even last throughout the subsequent Segment [B], the reader becoming a quiet spectator, watching David from somewhere in his room. Such outer image would probably only last until the first mention, in the subsequent sentence, of David's inner feelings of being sleepy and hollow. That mention locates the perceptual center inside David's body, eliciting enactment-imagery instead.
>
> (p. 288)

While deixis may set up one's relation to the environment, it seems that factors like sensorimotor verbs and embodiment could be more influential on the reader's relation to the narrator. This relation may have been affected by the task at hand, namely, drawing one's mental imagery. Perhaps this task foregrounds attention to the spatial relationships over, for example, inner feelings, and moves participants away from adopting the narrator's (sensorimotor) experiences, as might otherwise happen according to the quote above. In terms of Kuzmičová's (2014) work, the instructions may encourage an "outer stance" (see Chapter 2) that makes readers conscious of visualizing the scene. Hypothetically, this may have hindered participants in spontaneously perceiving the protagonist's experiences. Experimental instructions can become situational factors that distract readers from immersion (Green, Brock, & Kaufman, 2004). However, as is evident from the results, this does not apply to each and every participant; for every fragment, there were some able to adopt the narrator's perspective still, and even some that did so consistently no matter the fragment. Therefore, further examination of reading experience is essential for interpreting our findings, as personal (or other) factors evidently need to be included.

Lastly, there were more shifts in scenes than initially expected. Perhaps by explicitly mentioning that drawing multiple scenes was allowed in the instructions, participants were prompted to do so. Most shifts followed the text's description of events, for example, for Fragment 4 (*Farewell, My Lovely*, Raymond Chandler), in which the protagonist took clear steps. Namely, the protagonist drove the car, stopped the car, got out, walked along a small path, stopped walking, and then turned to go back. Half of the participants included most of these shifts, all showing the car and the protagonist outside it, walking along the path and/or back to the car, or getting attacked while outside the car. Other fragments evoked zooming in, as with both versions of Fragment 7 (*Nooit Meer Slapen*, Willem Frederik Hermans), where participants zoomed in on the described plaque and its text. Alternatively, another example is Fragment 8 (*Lijmen*, Willem Elsschot), where some participants zoomed in on the described man to show more details.

3.3.3 Physical References and Sensorimotor Verbs

To consider the effect of physical references and sensorimotor-related verbs, we first need to briefly compare the fragments based on these two key aspects. We therefore analyse whether the text describes the narrator as predominantly dynamic (described to be moving) or static (not moving). These consequently suggest some fragments to be more action-oriented and others more oriented towards inner life (see Section 2.4). Moreover, we recount if there are few or many words emphasizing the body (of the protagonist), movement, and/or the senses. Consequently, we calculate the proportion of body-/movement-/sensory-related words to total amount of words (of the original fragment), in order to quantitatively compare the fragments in this regard. The separate proportions are then taken together to form a final percentage of the amount of body-/movement-/sensory-related words in each fragment. Last, the selected words are provided for a transparent overview of this analysis (with translations in italics). Table 3.2 summarizes the results.

Let us recall that physical references and sensorimotor verbs were both assumed to aid visualization of the scene and possible immersion in the narrative. It may therefore be sensible to expect that high proportions would align with fragments that drew the reader closer to the narrator, presumably sharing that perspective as a way to immerse themselves in the story events. However, the opposite result surfaces here. The three fragments where a majority of readers adopted the narrator's viewpoint, as outlined in Table 3.1 earlier, were Fragment 6 (*Karakter*, Ferdinand Bordewijk), Fragment 7 (*Nooit Meer Slapen*, Frederik Hermans), and Fragment 8 (*Lijmen*, Enschot). To compare the two tables, we need to add the proportion of a particular viewpoint for both the original and the manipulated version together in Table 3.1, as we did in the table above. After all, for this discussion, the perspective of the text (first-person or third-person) is not essential. Hence, that way Fragment 7 has 12 out of 20 participants adopting the narrator's viewpoint (still the majority).

Table 3.2 shows that these three (Fragment 6, 7, and 8) were the ones with the lowest percentage of body-/movement-/sensory-related words (respectively, 7.5%, 4.8%, and 2.9%). This would suggest that a focus on inner life or thought might actually encourage a shared viewpoint more so than a focus on physicality, movement, or sensory perceptions, contrary to the presumptions in Chapter 2. The physical and sensorimotor proportion scores of Fragment 6, 7, and 8 decrease consistently, consistent with their increasing focus on inner reflection. Fragment 6 is characterized by an almost absent narrator, who is mentioned only once in this section (with the pronoun "he"). The events seem to "just" happen; for example, the author did not have the narrator open the door, but chose to state "the door opened" instead. Fragment 7 then includes somewhat more narrator presence, but also a mental question the protagonist asks himself. Hence, this fragment draws attention to his thoughts more so than Fragment 6 did. Fragment 8 does this even more so, by having the protagonist clearly lost in thoughts, trying to remember where he knew the other man from. Here too, there is a mental question that only the protagonist and the reader can be aware of.

The fragments that resulted in readers perceiving a viewpoint from somewhat further away all ranged between 11.7% and 14.2% concerning their body-/movement-/sensory-related words percentage, distinctly higher than the fragments previously discussed. This further supports that higher proportions of physical references and sensorimotor words appear to motivate a mental viewpoint more distanced from the narrator. Naturally, we also consider the limitations of our current set-up as previously discussed,

Table 3.2 Overview per fragment (taking the original and manipulated versions together) of the narrator dynamics, the proportion of physical and sensorimotor references, and references in question

Fragment	Narrator dynamics	Proportion of body-/movement-/sensory-related words to total amount of words	Selection of body-/movement-/sensory-related words
1 and 1M – **Garden of Eden**, Ernest Hemingway	**Static**: protagonist is seated, in the act of reading	Body: 3/32 Movement: 1/32 Senses: 0/32 **Total: 12.5 %**	-shoulders, back, head -blowing through
2 – **The Crow Road**, Iain Banks	**Static**: protagonist is mostly resting and waiting	Body: 3/162 Movement: 12/162 Senses: 8/162 **Total: 14.2 %**	-arms, deep breath, smiled -tumbling, piled, surged, flitted, zoomed, turned, swept, hurrying, catch up, turned away, went, pick up -looked, taste, silently, the view, soft, dark, tasted, sweet
3 and 3M – **Jane Eyre**, Charlotte Brontë	**Dynamic**: protagonist is going into a room and mounting into a window seat	Body: 2/60 Movement: 5/60 Senses: 0/60 **Total: 11.7 %**	-feet, cross-legged -slipped, possessed, mounted, gathering, having drawn
4 – **Farewell, My Lovely**, Raymond Chandler	**Dynamic**: protagonist is driving and walking (alternating actions relatively quick after one another)	Body: 2/176 Movement: 11/176 Senses: 8/176 **Total: 11.9 %**	-head, head -drove, stopped, switched off, whispered, got out, walked, stopped, turned, whispered, movement, hit -quiet, lights, dark, dark, listening, sound, heard, sound
5 and 5M – **De Vergaderzaal**, Albert Alberts	**Static**: protagonist is standing and looking out of the window	Body: 1/31 Movement: 1/31 Senses: 2/31 **Total: 12.9 %**	-rug (*back*) -verdelen (*distributing*) - keek (*looked*), hoorde (*heard*)

(*Continued*)

Table 3.2 (Continued)

Fragment	Narrator dynamics	Proportion of body-/movement-/sensory-related words to total amount of words	Selection of body-/movement-/sensory-related words
6 – *Karakter*, Ferdinand Bordewijk	**Ambiguous**: protagonist clearly relocates but is not described doing so at all	Body: 0/93 Movement: 3/93 Senses: 4/93 **Total: 7.5 %**	-liep omhoog (*ascended*), leidend (*leading*), ging open (*opened*) -zwaar (*thickly*), licht (*light*), zag (*saw*), zware (*deep*)
7 and 7M – *Nooit Meer Slapen*, Willem Frederik Hermans	**Dynamic**: protagonist is walking	Body: 0/42 Movement: 1/42 Senses: 1/42 **Total: 4.8 %**	-loop (*walk*) -zie (*looking*)
8 – *Lijmen*, Willem Elsschot	**Static**: protagonist is seated, thinking	Body: 0/105 Movement: 1/105 Senses: 2/105 **Total: 2.9 %**	-afwenden (avert) -aangekeken (*looked*), blik (*gaze*)

namely, length and context. The current fragments diverge significantly regarding their amount of words, which affects the proportions in our analysis. We cannot guarantee that similar results surface for extracts of equal length. Likewise, we must recognize we selected a snippet; this current description could be interpreted differently when read in its normal context (a book). Nevertheless, these considerations of length and context were not incorporated in the discussions on the effect of language we outlined in Chapter 1. Therefore, for the purpose of our particular study (investigating the claims of researchers like Fowler or like cognitive stylisticians), the results are relevant and informative.

Including the idea of a static or dynamic narrator in this analysis, this categorization does not appear to affect the perceived viewpoint in any way. Namely, the three fragments eliciting a majority of readers to view the scene through the narrator's eyes had a mix of dynamics, making it unlikely that this had a consistent effect. Likewise, those texts encouraging a viewpoint from further away varied in their dynamics as well.

3.3.4 Schemas

A striking occurrence was the inclusion of objects not mentioned in the text, but conceptually related to the described scene, as found in related studies as well (Krasny & Sadoski, 2008). In Fragment 1 and 1M (*The Garden of Eden*, Ernest Hemingway), one participant added a desk, another a lighthouse, and a few included curtains and/or doors. For Fragment 2 (*The Crow Road*, Iain Banks), mountains were included in the background on two occasions. Fragment 3 and 3M (*Jane Eyre*, Charlotte Brontë) had three participants adding an easel and/or drawing, probably prompted by the words "drawing-room" or perhaps "pictures," even though neither term directly referred to painting supplies. The first relates to a specific type of room for receiving visitors, and the second to illustrations in a book. Most likely, this misconception stems from a lack of knowledge of what exactly a "drawing-room" is, potentially due to a language barrier or because the term is somewhat old-fashioned. In this same fragment, many participants drew a table and/or chairs, although these were not mentioned anywhere in the text. Likely, the term "breakfast room" elicited these, which one might expect includes such furniture. Some participants even included plates, cutlery, glasses, or a lamp. For Fragment 4 (*Farewell, My Lovely*, Raymond Chandler), some included trees, and one participant was presumably led by the potentially female-sounding name "Mariott" to believe this character was a woman. In Fragment 5 and 5M (*De Vergaderzaal*, Albert Alberts), the shape of the table varied as participants appeared to have varying connotations about what a "conference hall" looked like. Some had school-like associations, drawing multiple small desks in rows, while others imagined one big round table, and yet another group fell back on a prototypical square table. Evidently, the number of tables impacts the spatial relations significantly. Moreover, other details like a cup of coffee, clothing, or the view were drawn, again going beyond the descriptions within the text. Fragment 6 (*Karakter*, Ferdinand Bordewijk) similarly had additions such as paintings and carpets in the hallway, which could have well been there, but were not described. Likewise, for Fragment 7 and 7M (*Nooit Meer Slapen*, Willem Frederik Hermans) participants took it upon themselves to draw the buildings they assumed were in the background or to specify what type of stone covered the square. As for Fragment 8 (*Lijmen*, Willem Elsschot), some participants felt the need to indicate that the scene took place at a (fancy) restaurant, including aspects like suits, hats, ties, and again plates, cutlery, and glasses. None of these details was described, as the text only stated that the narrator was looking at a man sitting at the next table. Evidently, a stranger sitting at a table that is positioned at a certain distance or in a certain layout in relation to the narrator is enough to generate the idea of a restaurant or café setting. Still, as one participant imagined, the place could as well have been a bar.

The aforementioned examples show that schemas were activated that evoke expectations not mentioned by the narrative. Schema theory was advanced by psychologist Frederic Bartlett, who described a schema as an "active organisation of past reactions, or of past experiences" (Bartlett & Burt, 1933, p. 3). Another well-known influence in this field was the work of Schank and Abelson (1977), which describes how stereotyped sequences of actions may form a mental script. Moreover, there is the work of Fillmore (1975) and his frame semantics, which identified specific roles in certain events, e.g. buying and selling roles in a commercial event. Schemas, then, are abstract representations of meaning, built up by our everyday experiences (Bartlett & Burt, 1933; Fillmore, 1975; Evans & Green, 2006). These conceptual structures aid us in making sense of situations in daily life, e.g. by establishing certain expectations or roles. Repeated activities will entrench our schemas and form a script, while unexpected occurrences may broaden our schemas to encompass new associations. Thus, words are never understood independent of context, nor independent of the frame to which it is linked, as interpretation of language draws upon these structures.

Text may affect the activation of schemas in various ways. One influence is that a word or group of words can strongly suggest a particular schema, possibly activating it in its entirety (An, 2013). In Fragment 8, for example, the mention of a table opposite the narrator was sufficient for some to connect it to an entire (fancy) restaurant schema, including drinks, plates, cutlery, and appropriate clothing. Frequently though, only a certain slot is activated, which then can apply to multiple schemas (An, 2013), like how some participants interpreted "drawing-room" (Fragment 3 and 3M) in a more literal sense rather than a room to entertain guests, inspiring the connection to painting and thus to an easel. The word "drawing" filled the slot of drawing as an activity rather than being a type of room to withdraw to and that way elicited a different schema than likely intended by the author. For some drawings, these associations filled slots in a seemingly cascading manner. Some participants kept to simply drawing tables when a breakfast room or just another table was involved. Others then included plates or glasses, and yet another group then also added cutlery and/or candles. Perhaps for some just a plate already sufficiently represented the schema of having breakfast, while for others this included more slots, so to say. Then, there were participants who included clothes for the characters to match the setting (as the suits in Fragment 8) or to distinguish between genders through skirts, trousers, and long or short hair (sometimes mistakenly, as in Fragment 4 and Fragment 5). These accessories thus connected either to the schema of the setting or to the schema of gender, expressing for example the stereotypical idea that women have long hair. We should also consider the possibility that the act of drawing may have prompted participants to include more details (like clothes or cutlery), potentially to make it clear to the researchers what type of room they depicted. Another relation between text and schemas that An (2013) describes is that activated schemas may foreground connections between words that fit within the schema which otherwise would not have been made. If the textual cue of "conference hall" from Fragment 5 and 5M did not evoke a (strong) schema related to a business, words like "janitor," "notepads," or "pencils" may have elicited the schema of a school, possibly connecting "conference hall" to a school setting as just another meeting room. This may have prompted some participants to draw an arrangement that is more like a classroom, with multiple tables in even rows. Despite minimal instruction of the fragments regarding these features, schemas cause readers to fill in such details for themselves.

3.3.5 Preliminary Observations

It is appropriate to take stock of where we are regarding limitations, challenges, and preliminary recommendations before moving on to the more embodied and cognitive aspects of this study. As mentioned before, the drawing process itself might have interfered with the depiction of mental imagery. Participants might either not be capable of accurately representing the scene as they see it mentally, or distort certain aspects as a consequence of it needing to be drawn. Still, there are few reliable ways to access someone else's mental imagery; while some details likely were left out, the focus of this research is the relation between reader and narrator, so as long as that was clear, this was not a cause for concern. Some outcomes, however, appear to be somewhat ambiguous, for instance, when there was no depicted narrator. This could refer to either full immersion of the reader into the narrator position, or simply not perceiving a narrator in the scene. As mentioned, the length of the fragments might also have had an effect on our expected results. Possibly, these may have encouraged perspectives from outside the story world as opposed to readers adopting the narrator's experience. This then may have been reflected in the drawings in more perspectives from further away relative to sharing a viewpoint with the protagonist. On the positive side, the current time span did appear to cause participant motivation to remain high, and indeed various participants commented that the task was entertaining and pleasurable.

The two hypotheses outlined at the beginning of this chapter were that (H1) the author's control of the reader's perception would be strict and dependent on linguistic artifices, or that (H2) the author's control of the reader's perception is not strict and not dependent on linguistic artifices. The results in this chapter provide provisional support for both, as there are remarkable similarities across participants for each fragment, as well as significant differences.

Overall, underlying H1, every fragment had a majority interpretation, meaning that each time more than half the participants aligned with regards to how they drew the general spatial organization of the scene or general layout. Besides this considerable overlap between drawings of each fragment, there was also overlap between original and manipulated fragments, with some variations being relatively minor (e.g. whether a view through the window was possible, which side of a statue was shown/visible, or whether a bookcase was in the same room or not). In support of H2, all fragments had at least two (up to four) subgroups, supporting at least some diversity in layout for each fragment. Moreover, some subgroups were strikingly different, such as for Fragment 5 and 5M (*De Vergaderzaal*, Albert Alberts), where some placed the viewpoint outside the room altogether. In even a relatively small group of ten participants, the diversity was telling. Furthermore, the participants filled in details not mentioned in the fragments, likely prompted by their schematic knowledge of the described environments. Some additional details were minor (e.g. a lamp or painting in a room), but some concerned the very nature of the setting (e.g. being a restaurant or a bar).

Some of the variations described in the results should be considered with care. For Fragment 2 (*The Crow Road*, Iain Banks), one may have noticed there were quite some variations regarding the positioning of the river relative to e.g. the forest within a grouping. There were also variations in the majority group of Fragment 4 (*Farewell, My Lovely*, Raymond Chandler), concerning the direction of the road or the placement of the ocean. It is fair to note here that some fragments do not explicitly mention the spatial relations of all its elements. The key observation in our analysis for Fragment 2 is therefore also the positioning of the narrator in relation to the larger view, rather than the constituent elements of that view. This is to emphasize that the placement of the elements should be analysed in relation to one another more so than in relation to the page (e.g. being on the left or right side of the canvas). Moreover, for the drawings interpreting details not described in the scene, similar caution may be applicable. One example is the shape of the furniture, e.g. whether participants drew round or square tables. While such variations show differences in imagination and evocation of schemas, this impacted spatial relations only in some cases. If the text does not describe shape, it is forgivable that readers could opt for one shape or the other. The most compelling aspect is then the underlying factors that prompt them to decide, which Chapter 4 aims to investigate further. Last, there were also objects that were included while not outlined in the fragment. In those cases, context could have been crucial; it could be elements that would have been described previously or would be described later where more context is provided. For example, what room the protagonist finds himself in in Fragment 1 (*The Garden of Eden*, Ernest Hemingway) could resolve the ambiguity whether the furniture in the room is likely to be a bed, couch, chair, or window seat, or if the protagonist would be seated on the ground. Similarly, some participants indicated Fragment 8 (*Lijmen*, Willem Elsschot) to take place at a restaurant, yet this was not specified. Additional context would affect the way participants imagine the scene, and likewise variations such as including plates, other tables, other people, or "fancy" clothes or not. The build-up of this knowledge may be something that is normally under the author's control and aiding the mental construction of (recurrent) spaces but was simply not reflected in this experiment due to the length of the fragments. In other words, the decontextualization of the texts presented should be considered when analysing the current results.

Thus far, we have explored the impact of language and point of view on literary-induced mental imagery, in particular readers' mental viewpoints. To give a more rounded insight into these results and what might have influenced our participants while creating them, we consider the broader field of embodied cognition in Chapter 4. In particular, we explore in embodied cognitive terms what might be happening when literary readers envision a scene guided by language, as we have seen in the drawings of the participants in the study. Chapter 5 will then incorporate that information into a more in-depth discussion of the analysis provided here.

Notes

1 Translation: "The secretary stood by the corner window of the conference hall and looked outside. He heard how behind him the janitor was distributing notepads and pencils around the table."

2 Translation: "At the end of the hall, across its full width, a thickly carpeted, seven-stepped staircase ascended, leading to a massive eighteenth-century door. The door opened. In the light of a many crystalled chandelier, he saw, seated at a long, green table, a few red-faced gentlemen, veiled in thick cigar smoke. At the head of the table sat an old man with hair like that of a grey lion whose scruffy mane stands on end. An excited, deep voice said three times 'Absolutely, absolutely, absolutely,' each time emphasizing the first syllable."

3 Translation: "In the middle of the square there stands a monument of blue copper; it's of a man in arctic clothing on a square pedestal. From where I stand, I am looking at his back. Who is he? I walk towards it and read the name that is written on the pedestal: ROALD AMUNDSEN."

4 Translation: "I had looked at that man, who was sitting at the next table opposite me, a few times already, because he roused memories in me, even though I knew for sure I had never met the likes of him. He looked successful and bourgeois, like a man of enterprise, and yet he reminded me of the Flemish lion flag and The Battle of the Golden Spurs, of young men with beards and felt hats. In his buttonhole there was a decoration and next to him, on the table, lay a pair of neat gloves. No, I had never associated with people of that sort, but, still, I could not avert my gaze from him. Where, where, where?"

5 That researcher in question was the first author of this book, Bien Klomberg.

4 Embodied Cognition and Point of View

4.1 Introduction

In this chapter, we will explore language and its connection to cognition and the principles of embodied cognition. We will also consider the notions of (i) private memories, (ii) sensory simulations, (iii) the simulation of others' minds, and (iv) how meaning-making is explained from the perspective of reading as a skill.

4.2 The Embodied Cognition Approach

Kuzmičová's (2014) categorizations of mental imagery experiences are informed by embodied cognition, a non-Cartesian cognitive science approach (Rowlands, 2010) gaining impetus widely (Barsalou, 2010) and becoming increasingly influential in disciplines concerned with meaning-making processes such as reading research (e.g. Gibbs & Colston, 2019; Mangen & Schilhab, 2012; Zwaan, 2009). The approach challenges static, representational understandings of cognition conceived as a mental activity decoupled from living life (Glenberg, 2015). Hence, embodied cognition opposes the conception that meaning-making in cognitive activities such as imagining when reading results from computations operating on representations isolated from experiential content (e.g. Foglia & Wilson, 2013). Instead, the approach holds that the minds of cognizers are always embodied, embedded, enacted, and extended (Menary, 2010; Rowlands, 2010; see also Rietveld et al., 2018). Consequently, an adequate understanding of cognitive processes in meaning-making activities must consider cognizers' bodies, surroundings, and continuous exchanges with those surroundings (Fuchs, 2017; Walter, 2009).[1]

One rather under-researched yet significant implication of the embodiment, enactment, and embeddedness perspectives of cognition is that cognitive processes are inherently subjectively biased (Schilhab, 2011). Accordingly, by

DOI: 10.4324/9781003225300-4

default, cognitive processes oppose a "view from nowhere," the term coined by philosopher Thomas Nagel (1989). For example, Zwaan and Madden (2005, p. 224) posit that former and current experiences are woven into the fabric of meaning-making in the present as so-called experiential traces, while Rucińska and Gallagher (2021) explicate how previous experiences constrain ongoing imaginative processes. In short, the meaning-making available to any meaning-maker when reading depends on their specific history of experiences, which we refer to here as simply "historicity." Consequently, the subjective perspective that suffuses the embodied approach informs explanations of the diverse reader interpretations presented in this work.

Guided by the historicity implications of the first-person perspective, we first present the central aspects of the embodied cognition approach to stipulate the sense in which language, as the central meaning-making vehicle in reading, is grounded in direct experiences. We emphasize the shift from processing language, as merely another behavioural aspect of situated meaning-making, to processing language in the sense of becoming the unique prism by which former experiential content is re-enacted.

Second, we point to the manifold cognitive processes in any moment of mental life as co-contributing to readers' divergent interpretations as well as the distinction between non-conscious and conscious processes, which are crucial when addressing meaning-making in reading. Given the significance of historicity, we suggest that the compound nature of experiential content constituting cognition is likely to result in private meaning-making processes that might cause readers' divergent interpretations and subsequent drawing activities presented here. To further unfold the significance of subjective experiences in interpretation and linguistic meaning-making, we discuss the relation between the particularity of first-person experiences and the development of expert knowledge.

To explain how readers' preferences for first- or third-person perspectives arise, we then turn to re-enactment processes in relation to the simulation of others' minds. Finally, we apply the idea of historicity and skill development underlying the embodied cognition framework to discuss meaning-making in reading. For that, we introduce Dreyfus and Dreyfus's (1980) skill acquisition model to tentatively explore how readers approach the meaning-making activity when processing text. We end by suggesting that readers' divergent interpretations and subsequent drawing activities presented here could result from the meaning-making competencies acquired by the individual.

4.3 Language and Its Connection to Cognition

The assertion that cognition is always embodied, enactive, embedded, and extended situates language acquisition as well as subsequent language processing in an experiential context in which linguistic meaning-making emerges as part of lived life. In early childhood, the acquisition of language is directly associated with lived experiences (Pulvermüller, 2005) in which the linguistic activity co-occurs, blends into, and co-constitutes meaningful socially framed whole-body experiences (Schilhab, Balling, & Kuzmicova, 2018; Trasmundi, Kokkola, Schilhab, & Mangen, 2021).

On the one hand, lived experiences carve out a conceptual understanding bottom-up through embodiment, situatedness, and enactment, which was coined as the process of "situated conceptualisation" by Barsalou (2009). In other words, you understand because living life following from being embodied and enacting in a given situation *is* the meaning. Meaning is what you experience while being alive. On the other hand, you conceptually understand because conceptual understanding emerges from the situations demarcated by certain bodily actions, social and physical environments, cultural interpretations, and linguistic actions (e.g. Galetzka, 2017).

For example, when children learn to conceptualize entities such as "cup," such learning typically occurs in a "drinking situation" where they are simultaneously senso-motorically and perceptually engaged by physical cups in a meaningful social drinking interaction. Although impossible to disentangle in reality, meaning-making in such drinking situations can be analytically decomposed into the (1) affective responses shared among the child and carer, (2) interoceptive state of the child, (3) odour, taste, and texture of the beverage offered, (4) micro-manipulation afforded by the cup, and, of course, (5) materiality of the cup itself. One might also include the (6) cultural significance of the event, (7) bodily position while drinking, (8) focus of the child's attention, and (9) precise order of words spoken, notwithstanding earlier experiences of such events (see e.g. Cowley, 2014; Sheckley & Bell, 2006 for presentation of some of these dimensions). For a systematic study of the colossal number of phenomenal categories available to conceptual understanding, see Binder et al. (2016).

Initially, the toddler in the drinking situation is potentially experiencing all the above aspects as co-constituting the symphony of meaning. Their significance to the child is likely to be determined by features like novelty and pleasure known to stimulate stimulus-dependent attention (Sood & Jones, 2013). Thus, the situational words spoken more or less constitutes the "verbal track" accompanying the composition. Gradually, the toddler is socialized into utilizing the same verbal track as their conceptual framing to associate the series of aspects that constitute the compound experience of meaning. The verbal track then functions as the "currency" that provides access to the original meaning and can be shared intersubjectively.[2] Hence, during language acquisition, spoken words shift status from co-constituting situated meaning to becoming the prism by which the individual may re-enact the entire situation. This shift was referred to as the "linguification process" by Schilhab (2015c, 2017a). As a result, subjects interpreting sentences as they read seem to re-enact the "real-life" case when attributing meaning to words (see Speed & Majid, 2020, however, for reflections about putative biases among the senses).

Such effects are demonstrated by Zwaan, Stanfield, and Yaxley (2002). In their study, subjects read sentences such as "the ranger saw the eagle in the sky" and "the ranger saw the eagle in its nest." Immediately thereafter, they were shown photographs of either an eagle flying in the sky or an eagle resting in its nest and asked to assess the degree of congruency between the object in the sentence and the object depicted in the photograph. In cases of congruency, the response time increased, leading the researchers to conclude that:

> the representation of meaning from linguistic input is a dynamic process involving malleable perceptual representations rather than the mechanical combination of discrete components of meaning.
>
> (p. 170)

Such findings are corroborated by the sensibility judgement study by Glenberg and Kashack (2002) in which subjects assessed the sensibility of a sentence such as "close the drawer." Subjects responded affirmatively by *pulling* or *pushing* a handle and thereby engaged in movements that would be compatible with or opposite the direction implied by the sentence. Response times fell significantly when subjects responded "yes" by pushing the handle and increased when "yes" was invoked by moving the handle in the opposite direction of that needed to close a physical drawer.

Another line of studies investigates which neural areas are recruited when reading about actual phenomena. In the study by González and colleagues (2006), subjects passively read words such as "cinnamon" and "garlic," which carry strong olfactory associations. The researchers found that the semantic processes were sustained by primary olfactory cortices normally active in the experiential processing of actual garlic and cinnamon. Thus, neurons that become active as a result of direct experiences with garlic or cinnamon also participate in the neural correlate corroborating the concept of garlic or cinnamon *without* the simultaneous presentation of the actual object.

However, the embodied cognition perspective can only explain a selection of relations between meaning-making and language (e.g. Mahon, 2015a, 2015b; Dove, 2016). The capacity for words and phrases to act as prisms for re-enacting real-life experiences applies especially well to utterances associated with everyday life (e.g. concrete phenomena, entities, and events available to the senses). Linguistic activities forming more sporadic associations with concrete phenomena, entities, and events likely reduce their quality as prisms (Borghi, Flumini, Cimatti, Marocco, & Scorolli, 2011; Borghi & Cimatti, 2012; Schilhab, 2018). For example, consider the rather few public criteria available when we assign experiential content to another person (Schilhab, 2002, 2015b, 2017a). In this case, it is not always obvious that we can infer particular mental states from particular events available to the senses.

Nevertheless, the fact that children begin life as linguistic meaning-makers in concrete contexts rich in experiences partly explains why learning a second language at school is often mastered with less command of language and less felt emotional intensity by the individual (e.g. Birba et al., 2020; Degner, Doycheva, & Wentura, 2012). When learners acquire their native language as part of meaning-making in lived situations, language meaning is saturated with various aspects of the situation. Here, meaning consists of emotional, embodied, enactive, embedded, and extended aspects (see Fernandino et al., 2015 for a study of the phenomenal qualities of concrete concepts). By comparison, teaching in class lacks the rich situatedness of one's native language, suggesting that re-enactments elicited by reading in one's primary language are richer than those elicited by reading texts in a second language (e.g. Kühne & Gianelli, 2019).

4.4 Private Memories

As touched on above, in principle, the number of co-constituting aspects cognitively accessible in any given meaning-making situation, reading or otherwise, is almost indefinite, as indicated in the following quote by Barsalou (2013, p. 2951):

> In a given situation, multiple networks implement parallel processing streams that perceive and conceptualize various elements of the situation, including the setting, self, other agents, objects, actions, events, interoceptive states, and mental states.

The variety of highly differing processes that feed into (or factually comprise) cognition at any given moment is important when discussing reading processes. First, analytically, we must separate the *perceptual* processes engaged by the present situation (online cognition) in the sense of active meaning-making processes from the *mental* processes engaged by re-enactions of situations not present (offline cognition) in the sense of using concepts to refer to offline situations or *imagining* in your mind's eye (e.g. Wilson, 2002; Gross et al., 2021). To grasp the processual differences between these cognitive actions, consider the following quote by Pearson, Deeprose, Wallace-Hadrill, Heyes, and Holmes (2013, p. 6):

First of all an image can be created directly from immediate perceptual information. For example, someone can look at a picture of a horse, create a mental image of the picture in their mind, and then maintain this mental image as they look away or close their eyes. Second, an image can be created entirely from previously stored information held in long-term memory. For example, someone can hear the word "horse" and then create mental imagery based on their previous experience of what a horse looks like.

Here, the cognitive processes are defined by whether the referent is physically present to the senses in a bottom-up fashion or imagined in a top-down fashion without any relevant immediate perceptual input (Schilhab, 2018). Since sensory processes (as implied by Barsalou's (2013) quote above) are entwined in numerous processes, including predictive top-down processes, the difference is a matter of degree.[3]

Consider how the reader is physically anchored in the moment when engaged in online cognition, while simultaneously immersed in the text when engaged in offline cognition (e.g. Mangen & Schilhab, 2012; Schilhab, Balling, & Kuzmicova, 2018). Similarly, meaning-making when reading is informed by the material feel of the reading device (Mangen, 2008; Schilhab & Walker, 2020), perception of the surroundings in which the reading act takes place (e.g. Kuzmičová, 2016), state and feel of the body when reading, and imagining prompted by the text (e.g. Schilhab et al., 2018; see Pearson, 2019 for a thorough discussion of visual mental imagery).

Recall the cognitive heterogeneity depicted in the quote by Barsalou (2013) that follows from the experiential nature of cognition. If, as posited, mental content is construed from a blend of parallel processes, which processes dominate the reader's mind in a phenomenal sense and why? As it stands, the quote by Barsalou (2013) includes no articulation of why some cognitive processes are consciously experienced in the mind's eye of the reader. However, individuals might sometimes become aware of parts of the processual stream (Barsalou, 2009, p. 1281): "When re-enactments reach awareness, they can be viewed as constituting mental imagery, given that imagery is typically assumed to be conscious." This quote distinguishes what is phenomenally present and therefore open to conscious cognitive operations in the mind of the cognizer from what is tacit and thus closed to consciously controlled cognitive operations.

When discussing the causes behind readers' divergent interpretations, we must explore further what decides the content of readers' minds. Barrett (2009, p. 330) describes how the *mental now* can be conceived of as an amalgamated construct:

Every moment of waking life, the human brain realizes mental states and actions by combining three sources of stimulation: sensory stimulation made available by and captured from the world outside the skin (the exteroceptive sensory array of light, vibrations, chemicals, etc.), sensory signals captured from within the body that holds the brain (somatovisceral stimulation, also called the interoceptive sensory array or the internal milieu), and prior experience that the brain makes available by the reactivation and reinhibition of sensory and motor neurons (i.e., memory). These three sources – sensations from the world, sensations from the body, and prior experience – are continually available, and they form three of the fundamental aspects of all mental life.

This tripartite division posited by Barrett's "cognitive moment" points us towards the putative causes for readers' cognitive biases when interpreting text fragments from either the first-person or the third-person perspective, making it plausible that they can be more or less inclined to read the snippets in this study based on either an exteroceptive or an interoceptive framing.

In fact, an fMRI study by Beilock, Lyons, Mattarella-Micke, Nusbaum, and Small (2008) has linked the primacy of the extero- or interoceptive perspective to the level of expertise and thus history of learning. The study monitors which neural areas were recruited while experienced hockey players, hockey watchers (with no hands-on experience), and novices assigned meanings to sentences about hockey. Subjects passively listened to sentences describing hockey actions such as "the hockey player finished the shot." The researchers conclude the following (p. 13272):

> The impact of athletic experience on comprehension is explained by greater involvement of brain regions that participate in higher-level action selection for those with hockey playing and watching experience and greater involvement of brain regions that participate in step-by-step action instantiation for those without such experience.

One implication of this finding is that when a trained hockey player understands hockey action sentences, areas related to physical activity are also recruited, preparing them for the actual physical events. Similar neural responses are not available to the novice because of the lack of associations of motor responses with linguistic material (see also Schilhab, 2011, 2017a). Hence, the degree to which the individual has experienced connections between physical movements and verbal tracks determines which neural counterparts are recruited when interpreting sentences.

The study of the neural corroboration of action imagery in experienced high jumpers and novices by Olsson, Jonsson, Larsson, and Nyberg (2008) further details the tight relation between motor experience and ability to re-enact first-person experiences. Here, the subjects were required to imagine their performance of a full jump, emphasizing certain stages such as take-off and clearing the bar. The instructions focused on first-person perspectives, nudging the participants to take an internal stance on imagination. Novices, who had no previous experience of the high jump, showed more activation of visual, occipital, and parietal areas, suggesting they were more inclined to view the task externally (i.e. watching high jumps from outside the action) because their previous experience was primarily as spectators (for further discussion, see Schilhab, 2017a).

According to Olsson and Nyberg (2010), the actual physical experience determines the perceived limitations of imagery with respect to both perspective and task complexity. From the perspective of embodied cognition, hockey and high jump novices have no practical knowledge (i.e. perceptual experience with the particularity of the actual situations) and therefore recruit different neural areas when performing such mental tasks (see also Paris-Alemany, La Touche, Gadea-Mateos, Cuenca-Martínez, & Suso-Martí, 2019). How does this pertain to the discussion on the reading study presented here?

As suggested by the hockey player and high jump studies, when subjects fail to assume the first-person (or third-person, when relevant) perspective intended by text fragments, the lack of first-person experience with the suggested action could be responsible. Although the above studies seem esoteric insofar as they refer to athletic expertise, their claims can be generalized to account for the differences in experience relating to all areas of learning, including cooking, driving in traffic (mentioned in Fragment 4), threading a needle, downloading files from the Internet, and cycling. Hence, subjects who have never ridden a bicycle will be less capable of imagining this activity from a first-person perspective. Moreover, subjects who have never repaired a flat tyre – including manipulating the inner tube, attaching the tyre levers to the rim, locating the hole in the tube, and keeping the tube submerged in a bucket of water –would address the activity from the third-person perspective.

Such claims are substantiated by the study conducted by Aziz-Zadeh, Sheng, Liew, and Damasio (2012), which describes how a motoric understanding of actions physically impossible for a subject to carry out is corroborated by alternative neural networks. For example, for the 58-year-old female subject of their study, a congenital amputee born without arms and legs, processing others' actions does not entail simulation processes. When observing actions by others that she could not perform herself, she "engage[s] more inferential processing to imagine others' states and intentions" (Aziz-Zadeh et al., 2012, p. 817; see Schilhab, 2017a for more in-depth discussion of this example; see also Schilhab, Fridgeirsdottir, & Allerup, 2010; Olsson & Nyberg, 2011).

4.4.1 Private Memories in the Context of Our Study

Hence, when the protagonist in Fragment 3 in our study exclaims that "I mounted into the window-seat: gathering up my feet, I sat cross-legged, like a Turk," a reader who knows about this cross-legged position exclusively from the third-person perspective may be more likely to draw the scene as an extrinsic experience. Comparable observations pertain to Fragment 8, with its references to the lion flag of Flanders (the "Flemish lion") and the "Battle of the Golden Spurs." Flemish people are more prone to adopt the first-person stance when reading this fragment given that they have similar embodied experiences to that of the narrator, which subjects of other nationalities have encountered only on rare occasions if at all, and never as a member of the Flemish community.

Likewise, Fragment 2 mentions the "spray [of the waterfall] was a taste" and "a deep breath that tasted of steam and the sweet sharpness of pine resin," which are uncommon sensory experiences. The oddity of these experiences may then help constitute extrinsic experiences accessed from an outside perspective.

However, due to imaginability, some linguistic descriptions may trigger first-person experiences in the reader *as if* he or she has had previous experiences of the sort even when that is not the case. In Fragment 5, readers may never have heard a janitor distribute notepads and pencils behind them, but they may have heard the sound of notepads and pencils being distributed around a table. Associating sound with specific actions (the sound of notepads and pencils around a table in this case) could be sufficient to invoke first-person sensations in the reader, thereby neglecting the idea of the janitor being present. It seems probable that many readers are likely to feel inclined to adopt the first-person perspective even when they experience a less-than-perfect match between the text and their re-enactments.

These considerations also pertain to Fragment 1. Here, the reading position depicted ("reading with his shoulders and the small of his back against two pillows") appears so general that a reader without any direct experience with the sea causing a breeze (for a description of a first-time experience at the age of five, see Collins, 2004) could easily visualize the scene from the building blocks referred to by the sentence, disregarding the fact that he or she could never re-enact a similar experience in their personal archive. Schachter et al. (2007) describe how imaginary scenes in our mind's eye are built from recombined details from past events (see also Hassabis & Maguire, 2009).

The ability to recombine what is described may explain the workings of sociocultural influences, where the object of the direct experience to be reenacted is either absent or more difficult to locate as a single phenomenon (see Schilhab, 2015a, 2017a for a related suggestion called "derived embodiment"). As an example, Fragment 7 describes a statue of Roald Amundsen, a Norwegian explorer. This description of a man in a polar outfit on a pedestal may be easily internalized using an immediate first-person interpretation by the majority of Norwegian readers. However, when reading this text, Danes, who have been widely exposed to Knud Rasmussen, the Danish arctic explorer, via narratives, television, historical accounts, and statues might be similarly engaged (e.g. Schilhab, 2007). Indeed, Danes are likely to visualize themselves seeing a statue of Knud Rasmussen, triggered by such phrases as "monument," "pedestal," and "man in polar clothing" irrespective of whether the reader realizes the text is about Roald Amundsen and not Knud Rasmussen. It seems probable that readers may thus entertain the sensation of embodiment concurrently by acknowledging that the reenacted feeling is merely analogous. In the next section, we explore this aspect further.

4.5 Mentalizing

So far, we have argued that the inclination to adopt either a first-person perspective or a third-person perspective when interpreting text fragments can depend on the scope of concrete experiences with the actions inferred. Now, we consult another strand of research also related to the embodied approach that could similarly explain readers' biases in adopting the first- or third-person perspective (e.g. Burke, Kuzmičová, Mangen, & Schilhab, 2016). Studies in social cognitive neuroscience suggest that the inclination to adopt the perspective of another person (i.e. to put ourselves in their shoes; Singer, 2006) "requires that one mentally simulates the other's perspective using one's own neural machinery" (Decety & Jackson, 2006, p. 54).

This activity may occur either involuntarily or voluntarily (Keysers, Meffert, & Gazzola, 2014; Ochsner et al., 2009). The involuntary variant is spontaneous and automatic (working bottom up) and is referred to as "emotional empathy." The voluntary variant is cognitive and reflective (working top-down) and is referred to as "cognitive empathy." Whereas emotional empathy typically entails sharing another person's emotional state (i.e. sensing what another person is sensing), cognitive empathy entails that the perceiver reflects on the perspective of that person while still keeping track of their own feelings as well as those of the other party (Decety & Jackson, 2004).

In concrete settings that are rich in perceptual cues, states of both emotional and cognitive empathy are likely to co-occur, although the extent of empathic responses in the empathizer is modulated by features like gender, personality, and mood (Engen & Singer, 2013). The empathic response has also been shown to depend on features of the relationship between empathizer and target, such as familiarity, affective link, and valuation of the other (ibid.). Intriguingly, in light of the historicity perspective on cognition pursued here, if empathizers have extensive experiences with pain-inflicting events in others, pertaining to for example physicians, their empathic brain responses are lower compared to the control group (Cheng et al., 2007).

When *reading* about the inner life of fictitious figures, external stimuli with the capacity to trigger emotional empathy are more or less missing, and readers are likely to actively engage in representation-based perspective-taking, which is a characteristic of cognitive empathy (e.g. Engen & Singer, 2013). Hence, lacking perceptual incentives in the environment to adopt the first-person perspective could explain why readers appear biased towards the third-person perspective as a default position when interpreting text fragments. Due to their lack of perceptual engagement, readers could be nudged towards the feeling of attending the described scene as an observer.

Similarly, it is highly likely that transportation and the feeling of immersion cannot be understood in the radical sense of entering a "mono-conscious" state. Even when people are absorbed in stories or films or concentrating on specific tasks, and therefore suppressing any perceptually felt awareness of their surroundings, they continue to monitor the external environment to some inobtrusive degree. Hence, readers' reports about feeling carried away and transported by narratives are likely to coexist with their background awareness of, for example, the physical existence of the reading material, their identity as the reader, the creative processes caused by the text, the time of day, whether they are dressed, and their name. This background awareness may also bias their preferred perspective in the sense that their default assumption is that they are spectators despite being simultaneously deeply moved by the text.

Importantly, in light of the historicity claim endorsed here, readers might be more used to reading materials from the third-person perspective than the first-person perspective. How often are readers assumed to read narratives from their own point of view? In other words, how common are narratives in which the preferred way of interpreting the story is to adopt the first-person perspective? Further, even if the use of that narrator technique is widespread, the story worlds of first-person narrators are still populated with "other people," which urges the reader to interpret the collection of characters from the third-person perspective despite full immersion into the narrator position.[4] However, in this study, readers were required to draw their perception of the scenes. It could then be argued that the anticipation of this act inclined subjects to both memorize and retract the memory in the visual mode, thereby accentuating those parts of the text that reflect the visual presentation of space. For example, when depicting Fragment 6, many subjects drew the grey lion mane even though they could similarly refer to the deep excited voice emphasizing the first syllable. From the perspective of drawing, the mane presents itself immediately, whereas drawing a voice taxes readers' ability to switch from imagining the scene in the auditory modality to representing the scene in the visual modality (e.g. Pecher, Zeelenberg, & Barsalou, 2003; Pecher, Boot, & Van Dantzig, 2011; Scerrati et al., 2015; Scerrati, Lugli, Nicoletti, & Borghi, 2016).

Recent studies suggest that the semantic parts of a narrative that readers are likely to simulate vary, indicating that they have preferences for particular aspects of a storyline. For instance, Nijhof and Willems (2015) report that participants who demonstrated high activity in neural areas concerned with mentalizing (anterior medial prefrontal cortex) when processing the mentalizing content of literary fiction scored lower on activity in the motor cortex when processing action-related content and vice versa. Likewise, in a study measuring eye-tracking, Mak and Willems (2019) investigate the roles of perceptual simulation, motor simulation, and mentalizing, which are related to aspects of story world absorption and story appreciation in individual reading behaviour. Thus, narratives may afford different simulation activities, with some readers being absorbed more readily into a story by mentalizing and others favouring simulating motor activity or perceptual experiences (see also Willems & Casasanto, 2011).

Of particular interest to this context is the fMRI study by Hartung, Hagoort, and Willems (2017) in which readers listened to two short fictional stories describing an event in the respective protagonist's life from either the first-person or the third-person perspective. Based on their phenomenological responses, the subjects were divided into three categories. "Enactors" scored high on the item, "At times, I had the feeling of seeing right through the eyes of the protagonist." Importantly, these subjects showed different neural activations from the second category of subjects – "observers" – who scored high on the question "During reading, I saw the situations in my mind as if I was an eyewitness." The final category of the subjects ("hypersimulators") simulated both the first-person and the third-person perspectives and shared activated networks with the other categories while listening. Likewise, Brunyé, Ditman, Giles, Holmes, and Taylor (2016) demonstrate differences in the extent to which the readers in their study adopted an agent's perspective in sentences using the pronoun "you" or "I." Readers who displayed a propensity to become more empathically engaged by the text were also more likely to adopt a first-person or third-person perspective. The propensity to adopt either the first-person or the third-person perspective may also arise from the strategies people pursue when they process experiences with a high emotional impact. Studies show that some subjects are prone to adopt a self-distanced bird's-eye view when processing negative emotions and experiences ("distanced why" strategy), thereby enabling the "cool" reflective processing of emotions (see also Schooler et al., 2011). This strategy helps them focus on the experience without reactivating excessively "hot" negative effects (e.g. Kross & Ayduk, 2009; Kross, Ayduk, & Mischel, 2005).

4.6 Historicity of Experiences and Reading Skills

The historicity of experiences and learning of skills have thus far been adopted as underlying assumptions that have guided the discussion of embodied cognition in reading. For example, the embodied cognition paradigm readily assumes that when neurons are systematically exposed to particular phenomena, events, or situations, they start to organize accordingly, known as "fire together, wire together," or Hebbian learning (e.g. Keysers & Gazzola, 2014). This tendency is expressed in traditional skill learning, such as musicians learning to play an instrument, high jumpers learning to jump their bars, and bicycle repairers learning to fix flat tyres. As detailed earlier, skill learning is essential for toddlers to become competent language users (Pulvermüller & Fadiga, 2010; Schilhab, 2015a, 2017a). At the neural level, skill learning depends on the similarities in particular (salient) aspects between learning episodes, which, due to the repeated activity of involved neurons, translates into strengthening the overall connection among neurons in the neural correlate to increase the signalling efficiency (Schilhab, 2017b, see also Draganski et al., 2004; Jäncke, 2009) due to the repeated activity of the involved neurons. The emerging automaticity and parallel increase in efficiency of task execution decrease the mental workload and liberate the mind for other tasks that demand conscious monitoring (although see Barreiros, Figueiredo, & Godinho, 2007 for contextual interference studies).

To identify what decides the content of the cognitive now in the reader's mind, we therefore suggest exploring the competency of meaning-making in reading from the perspective of skill learning. The relations between the development of automaticity, increase in the efficiency of task execution, and increased contemplative powers are extensively described in the skill acquisition model introduced by Dreyfus and Dreyfus (1980), which assumes that most skills are developed within a so-called problem field. Dreyfus and Dreyfus (1980) unfold the separate stages that lead to full-blown expertise in activities such as driving a car, playing chess, and working as a nurse. Problem fields are characterized by learning situations containing a wealth of potential information that affords numerous responses. For example, when a nurse attends a patient, he or she must navigate among a variety of cues at the same time and select the relevant ones to focus on in order to act appropriately. The stages leading to expertise begin at the novice level, where he or she is taught following explicit rules of the form "if X, then Y" that provide information about which acts to perform in relation to which cues.

At the beginning, when entering the learning arena, the problem field at the primary level (novice) appears almost without specific features, and the cues he or she must act on are superficial and easily recognizable for an outsider. In the second stage (advanced beginner), the nurse starts to grasp simple cue–action relations. Then, at the third level (competent), he or she starts to understand more complex connections as part of the cue–action relation. This nudges the nurse into becoming more invested, which leads to the internalization of parts of the problem field; therefore, their focus becomes defined by authentic judgements. At the next level (proficient), he or she will understand the problem field holistically and be able to prioritize aspects of the situation immediately. At the expertise level, the nurse reads the situation immediately and handles the task at hand seamlessly. Simultaneously, he or she even entertains her conscious understanding of the problem field as part of the holistic experience (see also Flyvberg, 1991).

As already implied, the skill acquisition model thus pertains to how to perform high jumps, play chess, and repair bicycle tyres. However, it applies equally well to skills such as mastering a language (as discussed by Collins & Evans, 2008) and as we suggest here learning to assign meaning to written language. Below, we unfold how Dreyfus and Dreyfus's (1980) model may explain readers' divergent interpretations when applied to reading skills.

When learning to read narratives, children must apply rules about how certain sounds are associated with particular letters. Later, they learn to recognize particular words based on the pattern of letters and ultimately when reaching proficiency they assign narrative meaning to the reading. This suggests that the mental activity sustaining early reading competencies is controlled by the application of rules, which may counteract abilities to obtain advanced imaginations from the reading act. However, at the other end of the expertise scale, expert readers like any skilled expert may be proficient in assigning meaning to the text by engaging with such tasks multiple times (e.g. Pacherie & Mylopoulos, 2020). On the abilities of expert chess masters, Dreyfus (2004, p. 180), for example, states:

> It has been estimated that an expert chess player can distinguish roughly 100,000 types of positions. For much expert performance, the number of classes of discriminable situations, built up on the basis of experience, must be comparatively large.

The expert reader bases their understanding of the text on hours and hours of experiences with texts, where the relation between first specific sounds with words and then words with meanings was trained. In the final stage, we hypothesize that the many hours of connecting text and meaning-making now frees the mind to juggle among versions of imagined interpretations smoothly. The characteristics of experts are described by Dreyfus (2004, p. 179) as follows:

> The proficient performer, immersed in the world of his or her skillful activity, sees what needs to be done but decides how to do it. The expert not only sees what needs to be achieved; thanks to his or her vast repertoire of situational discriminations, he or she also sees immediately how to achieve this goal.

When experts make subtle and refined discriminations within their problem field, they seem to be able to shuffle between different meaning-making scenarios on the spot. We suggest that expert readers experience a sense of flow not unlike flow experiences in expert bodily action that allows for certain types of awareness and conscious monitoring (Dow, 2017; Montero, 2015). Hence, in line with such considerations, the expert reader is characterized as using an agile approach to the skill of meaning-making. The versatile mind that juggles a number of scenarios can be illustrated by that of a grandmaster of chess that provides simultaneous displays blindfolded (see Schilhab, 2017a for this example). As part of the activity, the chess master memorizes the line-up pertaining to different games and switches between them at will. The cognitive burden of the task on novice players suggests that the capacity of the mind to switch smoothly between a variety of scenarios in the mind is a matter of expertise (see Shusterman, 2009 for a comparable case). The expertise of the chess master involves keeping an up-to-date record of the games and their particular objectives.

One could argue that reading exposes readers to similarly taxing problems. Smallwood, McSpadden, and Schooler (2008, p. 1144) state that:

> to make the best sense of the story, the reader must build a model that integrates general world knowledge with information from both

within and between different episodes in a narrative. In a process somewhat analogous to that of a detective, readers combine these disparate sources of information to create a *situation model* that denotes the cognitive representation of the narrative.

Hence, the expertise of the reader involves maintaining a number of situation models based on the forthgoing interpretation of the text. Similar conscious monitoring and mental adroitness is well known in the field of sports psychology, where "a 'mindful' moment-to-moment awareness and task relevant attention on current behavior" facilitates task execution in athletes (Vitali et al., 2019, p. 3; Toner & Moran, 2011). Based on the concept of expertise, it seems likely that competent readers differ in their ability to entertain particular elements of the situation model and may have slightly different versions of the situation model in their mind as they read. Some readers might excel in continuously testing their situation model while they read along, with other readers falling behind. Further, some readers might persevere with a particular interpretation of the situation model, while others revise their model continuously.

In line with the issue of non-conscious processing discussed earlier, consider that we only entertain a single track of thought consciously, whereas unconscious states can contribute several options in parallel. According to Strick, van Noorden, Ritskes, de Ruiter, and Dijksterhuis (2012, p. 1476):

> the capacity of the unconscious mind is, presumably, vast. Several different things can be accessible or temporarily primed at the same time (Wegner & Smart, 1997). That is, multiple thoughts can be unconsciously active simultaneously, for instance the answer to a question we were asked earlier that day (Yaniv & Meyer, 1987), the solution to a problem we have been mulling over for a while (Poincaré, 1913), the thought of a cold drink on a hot day (Aarts, Dijksterhuis, & De Vries, 2001), or an embarrassing memory we try to suppress (Wegner, 1994) can most likely all be accessible, but not conscious, simultaneously.

A competent reader does not consciously process every word to the letter (Gibbs & Colston, 2019). As discussed above, reading competencies entail the skill of acquiring meaning in a sweeping movement that seldom allows for the reader to dwell on every unit that makes up a text. Therefore, it seems unlikely that sentences are meticulously processed and recognized word by word. Words and phrases that for some reason are not consciously processed may still be influential at the subconscious level. Several meanings may thus reactivate and co-occur unbeknown to the reader. The following question then arises: to what extent do unconscious states "bleed" into the conscious stream of the reader and which parameters are responsible for this effect? An answer to this question is closely related to the notion of unconscious perception (e.g. Shepherd & Mylopoulos, 2021, Prinz, 2010, 2015; Phillips & Block, 2017).

According to transliminal research on the tendency for unconscious content to cross the threshold (Thalbourne, 2000), how easily unconscious states are converted to conscious states may differ per reader. Thalbourne (2009, p. 120) states:

> persons high in transliminality will, relatively speaking, experience a much larger number of different types of input from the subliminal regions, whereas others, lower in transliminality, may hear from that region on considerably fewer occasions.

4.7 Some Observations

First, it could then be argued that meaning-making in reading is highly dependent on the emergence of reading skills at an expert level, as depicted in the skill acquisition model. At this level, the reader is capable of shuffling between different meaning-making scenarios on the spot. Second, it could be argued that transliminal capacities (i.e. the ability to access the multiple thoughts that are unconsciously active simultaneously) are an important factor when we address perceived differences in readers' drawn point of view. Despite the initial unconscious status of the content, subjects with transliminal inclinations are more open to their internal stirrings than typical readers. In other words, they are characterized by "an openness or receptiveness to impulses and experiences whose sources are in preconscious (or unconscious) processes" ([Thalbourne, 1991, p. 181] in Thalbourne, 2000, p. 194).

Overall, we have argued that the embodiment, enactment, and embeddedness perspectives of cognition may very well explain some of the divergent reader drawings presented here. We have unfolded that from the embodied cognition perspective and the emphasis on direct experiences, it follows that cognitive processes are inherently subjectively biased (Schilhab, 2011). On that account, the meaning-making available to any meaning-maker when reading depends on their specific history of experiences, accentuating that meaning-making in reading is always also defined by the historicity of the individual.

Also, we have argued that the manifold cognitive processes in any moment of mental life – non-conscious as well as conscious – co-contributes to readers' divergent interpretations. The great variety of constitutive processes induces the possibility of ambiguity in any moment of mental life. Throughout the chapter we have pursued the implications of re-enactment and prediction which seem central to the emergence of the alleged historicity. We suggest that re-enacting previous experiences may be reflected in readers' preferences for first-person or third-person perspectives both when they simulate particular experiences like performing a high jump or when simulating others' minds.

Finally, we have applied the idea of historicity and skill development underlying the embodied cognition framework to discuss meaning-making in reading. And we have presented the case of transliminal readers to demonstrate that aspects like historicity, the manifold of processes in the moment, and skill learning in meaning-making activities such as reading are valuable concepts when addressing readers' interpretations in general. With all this in mind we now turn to our main discussion.

Notes

1 Instances of amodal, abstract, and arbitrary knowledge processing are reserved for select occasions (Mahon, 2015; Schilhab, 2017a). The embodied cognition field is heterogeneous though. Both weaker and stronger forms of the embodiment cognition formulation exist that differ with respect to the extent to which the body is also the realizer of cognition (Chatterjee, 2010; Chemero, 2011; Kiverstein & Rietveld, 2018; Meteyard et al., 2012; Rucińska & Gallagher, 2021; Varga & Heck, 2017).

2 Meaning and aspects are not to be understood in the static sense of these terms. At the neural level, for example, "meaning" is never fixed because every re-enactment changes the correlate (e.g. Rudy, 2008).

3 Barsalou (2009) clarifies this by stating that "when a perceptual stimulus activates a similar perceptual memory, the perceptual memory runs as a simulation of the stimulus and speeds its processing by activating relevant processing areas with the simulation perhaps fusing with the stimulus information" (p. 1286).

4 Future studies investigating readers who habitually read literature based on the first-person perspective could delineate the extent to which specific reading experiences support preferred perspectives when interpreting literature.

5 Discussion and Conclusion

5.1 Introduction

In this chapter, we bring our research question and hypotheses into dialogue with both our data from Chapter 3 and the studies that we discussed in Chapters 2 and 4, respectively. Our goal is to better understand what our data might mean. We also point to the possible implications of our research and we propose what kind of modifications might be made in future research in the area of literary language processing and mental imagery. We conclude with a short reflection on the original curiosity-driven question that gave rise to this study.

5.2 The Study

We started with Fowler's claim that "the author's control of the reader's perception – focus, survey, and scanning of relationships – is strict, and dependent on linguistics artifices which, though unobtrusive, are clearly defamiliarizing, since the language instructs us to perceive carefully, clearly, slowly, and relevantly" (1986, p. 165). We then showed how Fowler's theoretical assumption has been challenged by a large number of empirical studies that relied primarily on reader-response methodologies and that were working in the era of the cognitive turn of language processing. Thereafter, we generated two opposing hypotheses drawing on Fowler's terminology. The first (H1) was that the author's control of the reader's perception is strict and dependent on linguistic artifices. The second, opposing, hypothesis (H2) was that the author's control of the reader's perception is not strict and is not dependent on linguistic artifices. Then, based on our pre-study that emerged from a curiosity-based, informal experiment, we sought to test Fowler's claim using a methodology different from previous scholarship. Instead of using reader-response questionnaires or narratological theorizing, we employed the physical act of drawing in an empirical research

DOI: 10.4324/9781003225300-5

design. We then described a number of influential studies in the field of embodied cognitive science and neuroscience.

5.2.1 The Underlying Significance of Our Research

A number of relevant observations were made in Chapter 4 drawn from the research in the field of embodied cognition, which we synopsize here for the benefit of the discussion that will follow. First, we learned how the readers' divergent interpretations and subsequent drawing activities presented in our study are, in part, likely to result from private meaning-making processes. We saw further that these differences could also result from the meaning-making competencies that have been acquired by the individual. The research conducted by Zwaan, Stanfield, and Yaxley (2002, p. 170), for example, also illustrated how we get from language input to meaning during reading is not a predictable, automatic process involving delineated units of meaning. Rather, it concerns pliable and fluctuating representations that come together in an animated process.

We also learned from Barrett (2009, p. 330) that the different pictorial interpretations that are made by the readers in our study are likely to be constrained by three sources. These were sensory signals within the body, the physical condition outside the body, and the prior experience of the individual and their ability for recall. From this we can postulate that the variations in first-person and third-person perspectives in our drawn data could be accounted for by considering such "exteroceptive" or "interoceptive" framings.

Also in Chapter 4, we discussed a number of observations in the domain of "private memories." For example, from Fragment 3 in our study, knowledge of a cross-legged position, or regular experience of doing it yourself, may encourage a more third-person or first-person perspective when one is required to draw the position. This can be mitigated by the process of "imaginability," whereby an "as if" experience can be triggered in some readers irrespective of prior experience. The phenomenon of "derived embodiment" (Schilhab, 2015a, 2017a) that was discussed may also account for this.

The phenomenon of "mentalizing" was also touched on. Here we saw how the ability to mentally simulate the perspective of another was significant, both the involuntary kind, which generated emotional empathy, and the voluntary kind, which led to a more reasoned cognitive empathy (see Decety & Jackson, 2004 and 2006; Keysers, Meffert, & Gazzola, 2014; Ochsner et al., 2009). Here, we discussed how a lack of perceptual cues in reading experiences might favour a more third-person perspective rather than a first-person one, leading to a dominance of cognitive empathy. Furthermore, rich vivid drawing might be accounted for by the notion of "hypersimulators," as described in the fMRI studies of Hartung, Hagoort, and Willems (2017).

Some drawings in our study were unexpected, like the plan/layout distal depictions that some subjects produced. An answer for this may be found in the research of Schooler et al. (2011), who showed that individuals can adopt a distanced view, even a bird's-eye view, when confronted with representations that, owing to the person's prior experience, have a high emotive impact on that individual.

A final phenomenon that may impact the diversity of drawing in our study is the notion of "transliminality" (Thalbourne, 2000 and 2009), described in Chapter 4, whereby individuals can experience much more input from subliminal regions of the brain, thus plausibly leading to more varied and more detailed depictions in the context of our drawing data.

These empirical findings also find support in the more theoretical/philosophical accounts. It will be recalled from Chapter 2 how Mendelsund, in his discussion on "memory and fantasy" while reading, observed how much the mental imagery readers experience during reading is not tied to the text, and that literary texts invite our minds to both construe and to drift. He concludes from this that "reading imagination is loosely associative – but it is not random" (p. 296). He adds to this that the effect of words in literary texts does not reside in their semantic load but rather "in their latent potential to unlock the accumulated experience of the reader" (p. 302). Such words, he suggests are not inactive but are "brimming with pertinence" (p. 303). Similarly, in his discussion on the topic of "blurredness," Mendelsund observes how, when reading images, they will mainly consist of sketches, not particulars (p. 419). It can be observed that much of the data in our study supports these observations and contemplations on the topics of both "memory" and "blurredness."

The emphasis on experience is important. The desirable quality of reading is – according to Mendelsund – all about re-experiencing. However, it would be interesting to investigate how it still differs from actual experiencing. In contrast to real life, the reader is allowed to co-construct and dwell in the experiencing so as to fit their own mind. For example, reading may offer opportunities for dragging time, exploring what occurs in the mind's eye to a much larger extent than what is possible when experiencing by externally induced perception, thereby constructing mindscapes that are different from both what the author intended and the normal format of experiencing. These mindscapes depend both on the reader's previous experiences and their desires of where to travel mentally. That is – the pendulum (i.e. the imagery resulting in the reader) swings between (or is a conglomerate of) what the author prompts, and what the reader is willing to do (including involuntary associations) with the words that they have been offered. Readers may dwell on the sensations that significant words may leave with/in them and also follow up on these internally in their own time. Hence, reading is much more a dialogue unfolding between the author and the reader – but in which the reader can allow themselves to elaborate or refuse to accept the premises of the dialogue – partly because time is more fragmented than if the dialogue were taking place in real time.

In short, what we can conclude from all of the above is that when interpreting literary text fragments, language is not instructing or determining the imaging that takes place, as if a reader were "there" and that most of the divergence in the drawings that we have encountered in our data can plausibly be explained by such cognitive phenomena as embodiment, enactment, and embeddedness.

5.3 Implications, Limitations, and Further Research

Our study has implications and it also has opportunities that should be grasped in future research. We started to allude to these in the discussion in the previous section. Here we list them in order to create more clarity on extended and new research lines.

In the interim discussion at the end of Chapter 3, we deliberated on the post-experiment questionnaire. This survey yielded some valuable insights. Some of the comments aligned with our data and supported our discussion and some did not. Let us briefly look again at sections of the data and try to suffuse them with meaning for future studies. We look specifically at the two notions of language and drawing.

5.3.1 Language

With regard to language, the participants in the study were all English L2 speakers, although they studied at an English-speaking college (UCR) and several of them had enjoyed an English-speaking IB education. Nonetheless, this did not mean that they were native speakers and semantic nuance in the literary texts presented in the experiment may at times elude them. For example, two participants said they struggled with the language. One left the comment: "Honestly, I did not understand some of the words," which we speculated may have been the case for Fragment 3 and 3M (*Jane Eyre*, Charlotte Brontë) when a "drawing room" was described. This description namely resulted in three depictions (across both participant groups) of an easel and/or drawing, which led us to believe the original description had likely been misinterpreted. We did not follow up in this study on the importance of the L2 dimension for our data. Future studies might consider using Krasny and Sadoski's (2008) set-up of using translated texts as this would be valuable to further compare the influence of a first or second language on literary-induced mental imagery.

The dimensions of the texts that were used in the study are also something that we need to reflect on here. For example, the length of the text fragments may have affected the perceived viewpoints. A further consideration is that the decontextualized fragments that we employed for the experimental setting may be harder to interpret, since the reader is dropped into the narrative *in medias res* and therefore does not know the characters' or story's goals. Both these textual observations may lead to compelling questions for future research, which could test first-person fragments of varying lengths as well as present fragments with their story synopses in contrast to presenting them without context. In future studies, one might explore the relation between an increase of fragment length and greater immersion to see whether a positive relation exists between these factors.

A further aspect regarding language that should be considered in future research is the option of not only focusing on "neutral shading," to use Simpson's term, as we have here. Instead, one could generate other hypotheses, for example, that, owing to the differences in assurances and beliefs, positive shading may prompt perspectives originating from closer to the narrator (or adopting their point of view), whereas negative shading might prompt readers to view the scene from further away.

Another aspect tied to language that could be a significant variable is reader expertise: in effect, how much exposure to literature and to literary language might a person in the study have had. For example, across fragments, two participants imagined every text from a perspective further away and two imagined scenes solely from the narrator's perspective. For these four participants, the language of the text did not appear to affect their imagined viewpoints. Future studies may want to include readers' expertise and also their intrinsic motivation to investigate what kinds of characteristics may lead to consistent mental "stances," as opposed to readers who fluctuate or vary in their imagined viewpoints. Linked to the notion of expertise is the phenomenon of experience and, more specifically, physical experience. The studies reported in Chapter 4 (e.g. Schilhab, 2011, 2017a; Olsson, Jonsson, Larsson, & Nyberg, 2008; Olssen & Nyberg, 2010; etc.) on neural correlations and active physical experience attest to the importance of experience in reading, both reading sentences and imagining pictorial worlds. Also, with regard to empathy and perspective taking, future studies investigating readers who routinely read literature based on the first-person viewpoints could outline the extent to which specific reading experiences support favoured perspectives when interpreting literary texts.

Finally, maybe the mood of the reader or the location or indeed time of the reading event could all have had an influence on the drawings that were produced (Burke and Bon 2017; Bon and Burke forthcoming, 2022). These bodily and environmental aspects would straddle Barrett's earlier mentioned "interoceptive" and "exteroceptive" inputs (Barrett, 2009, p. 330).

These then are some observations with regard to the language aspect of our study. Let us now consider the physical act of drawing itself.

5.3.2 Drawing

The other most relevant set of comments in the post-experiment question-naire pertained to the act of drawing. Two participants struggled with draw-ing their mind's eye specifically, as one said: "one thing I found difficult is showing where exactly I was looking from, it ends up quite flat on the screen, it's hard to represent it spatially" and the other comment mentioned that "deciding what to leave out is hard." Pertaining to the first comment, as mentioned in the methods section of Chapter 3, participants were not trained in complex perspective drawing beforehand, so understandably, some participants will have lacked the skills to accurately create a detailed representation in their drawing. These skills are neither inherent nor easy, and in hindsight, these abilities may be necessary for some participants to confidently represent their mental image. Allowing simplified depictions, as we did, may not be sufficient to permit participants to adequately reflect the image that was in their minds. If they lack the reassurance that they are able to capture the actual mental image in drawing, then they might have simplified the spatial relations in order to be able to produce and repre-sent them. This course of action is implied by the second comment, which describes leaving out elements. This comment does not specify whether this concerns background aspects, e.g. street flagstones or a multitude of books in a bookcase, or indeed more prominent/foregrounded objects. The former would likely not affect the results in a significant way, but the latter should be guarded against. Therefore, we recommend that in future studies of this kind, drawing skills should be considered as a factor in future research or, preferably, be included in a pre-experiment training session.

Moreover, some differences between drawings were minimal. For exam-ple, we see this in Fragment 4 (*Farewell, My Lovely*) pertaining to whether the protagonist is in the car or is not. The protagonist in Figure 3.16 is not shown (with the exception of his hands in the bottom left-hand corner of the image), while Figure 3.14 shows the protagonist in full-body profile undertaking some action. This is related to how we made the classifications of subgroups: focusing on the visual and spatial elements. We should depict what we see (the protagonist in full or just their hands) and how they relate to the other entities that we imagine spatially.

The fact that there were more shifts in the drawings than were expected suggests that future research might record the drawing process of the participants and examine whether the order of drawing corresponds with the order that elements appear or are presented in the text. This would directly target Fowler's claims regarding spatial deixis and the ordering of the perception process. For example, Fragment 7 (*Nooit Meer Slapen*) mentions "a statue, a man in arctic clothing, on a pedestal," in that order. The question arises as to whether some participants then feel encouraged to draw the statue before the pedestal. If so, this would support the guiding function of deixis in the most explicit way. Of course, such a study would have to take into consideration the work conducted by Gibbs and Colston (2019), described in Chapter 4, that it is highly unlikely that readers process sentences meticulously, word for word, but instead that meaning is acquired in sweeping movements through the text. Eye-tracking methodologies may be one way to investigate this further, though the link from meaning to mental imagery would have to be strengthened first.

The drawing capability of the reader as compared to the scene is important. What does it mean to draw a scene? Why are so many respondents also writing things down if not because they felt inadequate when doing the drawings? How does the instruction pertain to what the subjects felt and how well does the drawing convey what the subject felt? Also, does it matter whether a drawer/participant is right-handed or left-handed? Might this affect how drawn objects are represented in space both horizontally and vertically? A further idea for future study, pertaining to drawing, could be to video record the drawing process itself as this would target the guiding potentiality of deixis more specifically.

Another pertinent inquiry could be to investigate what it is that makes readers report about spatial circumstances in the text fragment. From the drawings, we saw how subjects tend to draw spatiality and to draw objects for obvious reasons. Might there be a particular bias in using drawing as a vehicle for the mental imagery? How does a subject in a study draw what something feels like? If a reader happens to be someone who is more concerned with the feelings/sensations that are elicited by the reading, how does that reader go about using the method of drawing to convey these feelings/sensations? If we reflect on text Fragment 2 (*The Crow Road*), for example, the atmosphere evoked by the owl, the darkness, the railway, etc., stretches out into the unknown. The fact that the readers often draw multiple scenes and use words for the purpose of clarification may point to the notion that it is difficult for them to draw their feelings and, further, that their feelings, as they immerse themselves in the story, are much more complex than what may be captured in a visual scene. Hence, it may show that the first-person/third-person point of view is helpful as a tool, but it does not, and cannot wholly, encompass what is happening in the mind of the reader. Indeed, the very act of relying wholly on visual data to account for what might be going on when readers read literary texts and experience mental imagery flies in the face of what the philosopher Hans Jonas argues in his work *The Nobility of Sight* (1954), namely, that we have learned to accept a worldview based on the visual sense, downplaying that the world speaks to us through all our senses. This is a potential restraint on our study.

Let us bring this discussion on language and drawing to a conclusion by returning to the two hypotheses outlined in Chapter 1, namely, that the author's control of the reader's perception would be strict and dependent on linguistic artifices (H1) and, the opposite, that the author's control of the reader's perception is not strict and not dependent on linguistic artifices (H2). The results outlined in Chapter 3 appeared to provide support for both hypotheses, since, as we explained at the end of Chapter 3 in an interim discussion, there appears to be a relatively significant number of similarities across participants for each fragment, as well as significant differences. However, if we review these interim observations, set against the background of the experimental data on embodied cognition discussed in Chapter 4, we see that the kind of "strict dependence/control" on words and linguistic articles (as set out in H1 and indeed what Fowler claimed) is almost certainly illusory. All of the representations deviate in some greater or lesser degree from the idea of linguistic "control" of the reader's perceptions. The varied types of evidence that have been gleaned from the experiments in the field of embodied cognitive science and neuroscience can account for most stages that appear on this "cline of pictorial variance and deviance." It is therefore not an either/or question, H1 or H2. All are essentially H2, but they appear on a continuum. These range from examples that appear to be "expected" to ones that are clearly unexpected, with more examples appearing at the upper, unexpected end of this cline, rather than at the lower, expected end.

5.4 Conclusion

We started this book with an anecdote based on the experience of one of us teaching an outdoor summer course on the bank of a river on the topic of "language, literature, and embodied cognition." The curiosity of that colleague led to a number of cumulative questions that have informed this study. The first was: What is it that readers see in their mind's eye when they read literature? The second, drawing on the research of Fowler, was: To what extent can the idea that "that the author's control of the reader's perception would be strict and dependent on linguistic artifices" still be accepted? The third was: Can a study that incorporates the very uncommon (in language studies, at least) act of drawing lend support to the large body of research-response studies and narrative studies conducted in the cognitive turn on the seemingly arbitrary relationship between language and the mental imagery it may or may not generate? With regard to this third question, we believe that we can state that our study does indeed support the claim that language does not control or instruct the mental perceptions of readers to see in an ordered and structured manner.

Drawing is a medium that few linguists, narratologists, and stylisticians have employed in their research and study designs when working on discourse processing experiments, be these literary or non-literary textual examples. Moreover, these three groups of scholars all too seldom work in interdisciplinary endeavours together with researchers outside the humanities, from such fields as psychology or neuroscience. We believe that this is a missed opportunity. We hope that our study, in spite of its limitations, may inspire some of those fellow scholars to venture down the visual path of drawing experimentation that we have taken here. The potential for new discoveries that can tell us more about how the mind works in language processing and mental imagery contexts is huge.

References

Adoniou, M. (2012). Drawing to support writing development in English language learners. *Language and Education, 27*(3), 1–17. doi:10.1080/09500782.2012.7 04047.

An, S. (2013). Schema theory in reading. *Theory and Practice in Language Studies, 3*(1), 130–134. doi:10.4304/tpls.3.1.130-134

Aziz-Zadeh, L., Sheng, T., Liew, S. L., & Damasio, H. (2012). Understanding otherness: The neural bases of action comprehension and pain empathy in a congenital amputee. *Cerebral Cortex, 22*(4), 811–819.

Barreiros, J., Figueiredo, T., & Godinho, M. (2007). The contextual interference effect in applied settings. *European Physical Education Review, 13*(2), 195–208.

Barrett, L. F. (2009). The future of psychology: Connecting mind to brain. *Perspectives on Psychological Science, 4*(4), 326–339.

Barsalou, L. W. (2009). Simulation, situated conceptualization, and prediction. *Philosophical Transactions of the Royal Society of London B: Biological Sciences, 364*(1521), 1281–1289.

Barsalou, L. W. (2010). Grounded cognition: Past, present, and future. *Topics in Cognitive Science, 2*(4), 716–724.

Barsalou, L. W. (2013). Mirroring as pattern completion inferences within situated conceptualizations. *Cortex, 49*(10), 2951–2953.

Bartlett, F. C., & Burt, C. (1933). Remembering: A study in experimental and social psychology. *British Journal of Educational Psychology, 3*(2), 187–192. doi:10.1111/j.2044-8279.1933.tb02913.x.

Beilock, S. L., Lyons, I. M., Mattarella-Micke, A., Nusbaum, H. C., & Small, S. L. (2008). Sports experience changes the neural processing of action language. *PNAS, 105*(36), 13269–13273.

Binder, J. R., Conant, L. L., Humphries, C. J., Fernandino, L., Simons, S. B., Aguilar, M., & Desai, R. H. (2016). Toward a brain-based componential semantic representation. *Cognitive Neuropsychology, 33*(3–4), 130–174.

Birba, A., Beltrán, D., Caro, M. M., Trevisan, P., Kogan, B., Sedeño, L., ... & García, A. M. (2020). Motor-system dynamics during naturalistic reading of action narratives in first and second language. *Neuroimage, 216*, 116820.

Bon, E. V., & Burke, M. (forthcoming, 2022). Devices, settings and distractions: A study into how students read literature. In G. Watson & S. Zyngier (Eds.), *Pedagogical stylistics in the 21st century*. London: Palgrave Macmillan.

Borghi, A. M., & Cimatti, F. (2012). Words are not just words: The social acquisition of abstract words. *RIFL*, *5*, 22–37.

Borghi, A. M., Flumini, A., Cimatti, F., Marocco, D., & Scorolli, C. (2011). Manipulating objects and telling words: A study on concrete and abstract words acquisition. *Frontiers in Psychology*, *2*, 1–14.

Brunyé, T. T., Ditman, T., Giles, G. E., Holmes, A., & Taylor, H. A. (2016). Mentally simulating narrative perspective is not universal or necessary for language comprehension. *Journal of Experimental Psychology: Learning, Memory, and Cognition*, *42*(10), 1592–1605.

Burke, M. (2011). *Literary reading, cognition and emotion: An exploration of the oceanic mind*. London and New York: Routledge.

Burke, M., Kuzmičová, A., Mangen, A., & Schilhab, T. (2016). Empathy at the confluence of neuroscience and empirical literary studies. *Scientific Study of Literature*, *6*(1), 6–41.

Burke, M. & Bon, E. V. (2017). The locations and means of literary reading. In S. Csabi (Ed.), *Expressive minds and artistic creations: Studies in cognitive poetics* (pp. 205–232). Oxford and New York: Oxford University Press.

Caldwell, H., & Moore, B. (1991). The art of writing: Drawing as preparation for narrative writing in the primary grades. *Studies in Art Education*, *32*(4), 207–219. doi:10.2307/1320873

Chatterjee, A. (2010). Disembodying cognition. *Language and Cognition*, *2*(1), 79–116.

Chemero, A. (2011). *Radical embodied cognitive science*. Cambridge, MA: MIT Press.

Cheng, Y., Lin, C. P., Liu, H. L., Hsu, Y. Y., Lim, K. E., Hung, D., & Decety, J. (2007). Expertise modulates the perception of pain in others. *Current Biology*, *17*(19), 1708–1713.

Cohn, N. (2013). *The visual language of comics: Introduction to the structure and cognition of sequential images*. London: Bloomsbury Academic.

Collins, H. (2004). Interactional expertise as a third kind of knowledge. *Phenomenology and the Cognitive Sciences*, *3*(2), 125–143.

Collins, H., & Evans, R. (2008). *Rethinking expertise*. Chicago, IL: University of Chicago Press.

Cowley, S. J. (2014). Linguistic embodiment and verbal constraints: Human cognition and the scales of time. *Frontiers in Psychology*, *5*, 1085.

Culpeper, J., & Fernandez-Quintanilla, C. (2017). Fictional characterisation. In M. A. Locher & A. H. Jucker (Eds.), *Pragmatics of fiction* (pp. 93–128). Berlin: De Gruyter Mouton. doi:10.1515/9783110431094-004.

Decety, J., & Jackson, P. L. (2004). The functional architecture of human empathy. *Behavioral and Cognitive Neuroscience Reviews*, *3*(2), 71–100.

Decety, J., & Jackson, P. L. (2006). A social-neuroscience perspective on empathy. *Current Directions in Psychological Science*, *15*(2), 54–58.

Degner, J., Doycheva, C., & Wentura, D. (2012). It matters how much you talk: On the automaticity of affective connotations of first and second language words. *Bilingualism: Language and Cognition, 15*(1), 181–189.

Diessel, H. (2012). Deixis and demonstratives. In C. Maienborn, K. von Heusinger, & P. Portner (Eds.), *Semantics: An international handbook of natural language meaning, 3* (pp. 2407–2431). Berlin: Mouton de Gruyter.

Dow, J. M. (2017). Just doing what I do: On the awareness of fluent agency. *Phenomenology and the Cognitive Sciences, 16*(1), 155–177.

Dove, G. (2016). Three symbol ungrounding problems: Abstract concepts and the future of embodied cognition. *Psychonomic Bulletin & Review, 23*(4), 1109–1121.

Draganski, B., Gaser, C., Busch, V., Schuierer, G., Bogdahn, U., & May, A. (2004). Changes in grey matter induced by training. *Nature, 427*(6972), 311–312.

Dreyfus, S. E. (2004). The five-stage model of adult skill acquisition. *Bulletin of Science, Technology & Society, 24*(3), 177–181.

Dreyfus, S. E., & Dreyfus, H. L. (1980). *A five-stage model of the mental activities involved in directed skill acquisition.* University of California, Berkeley, CA: Operations Research Center.

Duchan, J. F., Bruder, G. A., & Hewitt, L. E. (Eds.). (1995). *Deixis in narrative: A cognitive science perspective.* Hillsdale, NJ: Lawrence Erlbaum.

Emmott, C. (1997). *Narrative comprehension: A discourse perspective.* Oxford: Oxford University Press.

Engen, H. G., & Singer, T. (2013). Empathy circuits. *Current Opinion in Neurobiology, 23*(2), 275–282.

Evans, V., & Green, M. (2006). The encyclopaedic view of meaning. In *Cognitive linguistics* (pp. 206–247). Edinburgh: Edinburgh University.

Fernandino, L., Humphries, C. J., Seidenberg, M. S., Gross, W. L., Conant, L. L., & Binder, J. R. (2015). Predicting brain activation patterns associated with individual lexical concepts based on five sensory-motor attributes. *Neuropsychologia, 76*, 17–26.

Fillmore, C. J. (1975a). An alternative to checklist theories of meaning. *Annual Meeting of the Berkeley Linguistics Society, 1*, 123–131. doi:10.3765/bls.v1i0.2315.

Fillmore, C. J. (1975b). *Santa Cruz lectures on deixis.* Bloomington: Indiana University Linguistics Club.

Fillmore, C. J. (1982). Towards a descriptive framework for spatial deixis. In R. J. Jarvella & W. Klein (Eds.), *Speech, place and action: Studies in deixis and related topics* (pp. 31–59). New York: John Wiley & Sons.

Fillmore, C. J. (1997). *Lectures on deixis.* Stanford, CA: CSLI Publications.

Flyvbjerg, B. (1991). *Rationalitet og magt: Bd. 1: Det konkretes videnskab; Bd. 2: Et case-baseret studie af planlægning, politik og modernitet.* Copenhagen: Akademisk forlag.

Foglia, L., & Wilson, R. A. (2013). Embodied cognition. *Wiley Interdisciplinary Reviews: Cognitive Science, 4*(3), 319–325.

Fowler, R. (1996). *Linguistic criticism* (2nd ed.). Oxford: Oxford University Press.

Fuchs, T. (2017). *Ecology of the brain: The phenomenology and biology of the embodied mind*. Oxford: Oxford University Press.

Galetzka, C. (2017). The story so far: How embodied cognition advances our understanding of meaning-making. *Frontiers in Psychology, 8*, 1315.

Gambrell, L. (1982). Induced mental imagery and the text prediction performance of first and third graders. In J. A. Niles & L. A. Harris (Eds.), *New inquiries in reading research and instruction* (pp. 131–135). Thirty-First Yearbook of the National Reading Conference. Rochester, NY: National Reading Conference.

Genette, G. (1972). *Figures III*. Paris: Éditions du Seuil.

Genette, G. (1980). *Narrative discourse: An essay in method*. Ithaca, NY: Cornell University Press.

Gibbs, R. W., Jr., & Colston, H. L. (2019). What psycholinguistic studies ignore about literary experience. *Scientific Study of Literature, 9*(1), 72–103.

Gibbons, A., & Whitely, S. (2018). *Contemporary stylistics: Language, cognition, interpretation*. Edinburgh: Edinburgh University Press.

Glenberg, A. M. (2015). Few believe the world is flat: How embodiment is changing the scientific understanding of cognition. *Canadian Journal of Experimental Psychology/Revue canadienne de psychologie expérimentale, 69*(2), 165–171.

Glenberg, A. M., & Kashack, M. P. (2002). Grounding language in action. *Psychonomic Bulletin & Review, 9*(3), 558–565.

González, J., Barros-Loscertales, A., Pulvermüller, F., Meseguer, V., Sanjuán, A., Belloch, V., & Ávila, C. (2006). Reading cinnamon activates olfactory brain regions. *Neuroimage, 32*(2), 906–912.

Green, K. (1992). Deixis and the poetic persona. *Language and Literature: International Journal of Stylistics, 1*(2), 121–134. doi:10.1177/096394709200100203.

Green, M. C., Brock, T. C., & Kaufman, G. F. (2004). Understanding media enjoyment: The role of transportation into narrative worlds. *Communication Theory, 14*(4), 311–327. doi:10.1111/j.1468-2885.2004.tb00317.x.

Grennan, S. (2017). *A theory of narrative drawing*. London: Palgrave Macmillan. doi:10.1057/978-1-137-51844-6.

Gross, M. E., Smith, A. P., Graveline, Y. M., Beaty, R. E., Schooler, J. W., & Seli, P. (2021). Comparing the phenomenological qualities of stimulus-independent thought, stimulus-dependent thought and dreams using experience sampling. *Philosophical Transactions of the Royal Society B, 376*(1817), 20190694.

Grünbaum, T. (2007). Action between plot and discourse. *Semiotica, 2007*(165), 295–314. doi:10.1515/sem.2007.045.

Hartung, F., Hagoort, P., & Willems, R. M. (2017). Readers select a comprehension mode independent of pronoun: Evidence from fMRI during narrative comprehension. *Brain and Language, 170*, 29–38.

Hassabis, D., & Maguire, E. A. (2009). The construction system of the brain. *Philosophical Transactions of the Royal Society B: Biological Sciences, 364*(1521), 1263–1271.

Herman, D. (1994). Textual *you* and double deixis in Edna O'Brien's *A Pagan Place. Style, 23*(3), 378–410.

Herman, D. (2002). *Story logic: Problems and possibilities of narratives*. Lincoln, NE: University of Nebraska Press.

Herman, D. (2014). Cognitive narratology. In P. Hühn, J. C. Meister, J. Pier, & W. Schmid (Eds.), *Handbook of narratology* (pp. 46–64). Boston: De Gruyter. doi:10.1515/9783110316469.46

Herman, D., Jahn, M. and Ryan, M.-L. (2005). *The Routledge encyclopaedia of narrative theory*. London: Routledge.

Jacobs, A. M. (2015). Neurocognitive poetics: Methods and models for investigating the neuronal and cognitive- affective bases of literature reception. *Frontiers in Human Neuroscience, 9*, 186. doi:10.3389/fnhum.2015.00186.

Jacobs, A M., & Lüdke, J. (2017). Immersion into narrative and poetic worlds: A neurocognitive poetics perspective. In F. Hakemulder, M. M. Kuijpers, E. S. Tan, K. Bálint, & M. M. Doicaru (Eds.), *Narrative absorption* (pp. 49–68). Amsterdam: John Benjamins. doi:10.1075/lal.27.05jac

Jacobs, A. M., & Willems, R. M. (2018). The fictive brain: Neurocognitive correlates of engagement in literature. *Review of General Psychology, 22*(2), 147–160. doi:10.1037/gpr0000106

Jäncke, L. (2009). The plastic human brain. *Restorative Neurology and Neuroscience, 27*(5), 521–538.

Jonas, H. (1954). The ability of sight. *Philosophy and Phenomenological Research, 14*(4), 507–519.

Keysers, C., & Gazzola, V. (2014). Hebbian learning and predictive mirror neurons for actions, sensations and emotions. *Philosophical Transactions of the Royal Society B: Biological Sciences, 369*(1644), 20130175.

Keysers, C., Meffert, H., & Gazzola, V. (2014). Reply: Spontaneous versus deliberate vicarious representations: Different routes to empathy in psychopathy and autism. *Brain, 137*, 1–4.

Kiverstein, J. D., & Rietveld, E. (2018). Reconceiving representation-hungry cognition: Anecological-enactive proposal. *Adaptive Behavior, 26*(4), 147–163.

Krasny, K. A., & Sadoski, M. (2008). Mental imagery and affect in English/French bilingual readers: A cross-linguistic perspective. *Canadian Modern Language Review, 64*(3), 399–428. doi:10.3138/cmlr.64.3.399.

Kross, E., & Ayduk, O. (2009). Boundary conditions and buffering effects: Does depressive symptomatology moderate the effectiveness of distanced-analysis on facilitating adaptive self-reflection? *Journal of Research in Personality, 43*, 923–927.

Kross, E., Ayduk, O., & Mischel, W. (2005). When asking "why" does not hurt distinguishing rumination from reflective processing of negative emotions. *Psychological Science, 16*(9), 709–715.

Kühne, K., & Gianelli, C. (2019). Is embodied cognition bilingual? Current evidence and perspectives of the embodied cognition approach to bilingual language processing. *Frontiers in Psychology, 10*, 108.

Kuiken, D., Miall, D. S., & Sikora, S. (2004). Forms of self-implication in literary reading. *Poetics Today, 25*(2), 171–203. doi: 10.1215/03335372-25-2-171

Kurby, C. A., & Zacks, J. M. (2013). The activation of modality-specific representations during discourse processing. *Brain and Language, 126*(3), 338–349. doi:10.1016/j.bandl.2013.07.003.

134   References

Kuzmičová, A. (2014). Literary narrative and mental imagery: A view from embodied cognition. *Style*, *48*(3), 275–293.

Kuzmičová, A. (2012). Presence in the reading of literary narrative: A case for motor enactment. *Semiotica*, *2012*(189), 23–48. doi:10.1515/semi.2011.071.

Kuzmičová, A. (2016). Does it matter where you read? Situating narrative in physical environment. *Communication Theory*, *26*(3), 290–308.

Levinson, S. C. (1983). Deixis. In *Pragmatics (Cambridge textbooks in linguistics)* (pp. 54–94). Cambridge: Cambridge University Press.

Lyons, J. (1977). Deixis, space and time. In *Semantics* (pp. 636–724). Cambridge: Cambridge University Press. doi:10.1017/CBO9780511620614.008

Mahon, B. Z. (2015a). The burden of embodied cognition. *Canadian Journal of Experimental Psychology/Revue canadienne de psychologie expérimentale*, *69*(2), 172.

Mahon, B. Z. (2015b). What is embodied about cognition? *Language, Cognition and Neuroscience*, *30*(4), 420–429.

Mak, M., & Willems, R. M. (2019). Mental simulation during literary reading: Individual differences revealed with eye-tracking. *Language, Cognition and Neuroscience*, *34*(4), 511–535. doi: 10.1080/23273798.2018.1552007

Mangen, A. (2008). Hypertext fiction reading: Haptics and immersion. *Journal of Research in Reading*, *31*(4), 404–419.

Mangen, A., & Schilhab, T. (2012). An embodied view of reading: Theoretical considerations, empirical findings, and educational implications. In Synnøve Matre & Atle Skaftun (Eds.), *Skriv! Les!* (pp. 285–300). Trondheim: Akademika.

Marmolejo-Ramos, F., Elosúa, M. R., Gygax, P., Madden, C. J., & Mosquera Roa, S. (2009). Reading between the lines: The activation of background knowledge during text comprehension. *Pragmatics and Cognition*, *17*(1), 77–107. doi:10.1075/pc.17.1.03mar.

Martínez, M.-Á. (2018). *Storyworld possible selves*. Berlin and Boston: De Gruyter Mouton. doi:10.1515/9783110571028

McIntyre, D. (2006). *Point of view in plays: A cognitive stylistic approach to viewpoint in drama and other text-types*. Amsterdam: John Benjamins.

Menary, R. (2010). Introduction to the special issue on 4E cognition. *Phenomenology and the Cognitive Sciences*, *9*(4), 459–463.

Mendelsund, P. (2014). *What we see when we read*. New York: Vintage/Random House.

Meteyard, L., Cuadrado, S. R., Bahrami, B., & Vigliocco, G. (2012). Coming of age: A review of embodiment and the neuroscience of semantics. *Cortex*, *48*(7), 788–804.

Miall, D. S., & Kuiken, D. (2002). A feeling for fiction: Becoming what we behold. *Poeticst*, *30*(4), 221–241. doi: 10.1016/S0304-422X(02)00011-6

Montero, B. G. (2015). Thinking in the zone: The expert mind in action. *The Southern Journal of Philosophy*, *53*, 126–140.

Nagel, T. (1989). *The view from nowhere*. Oxford: Oxford University Press.

Neary, C. (2014). Stylistics, point of view and modality. In M. Burke (Ed.), *The Routledge handbook of stylistics* (pp. 175–190). London: Routledge.

Nijhof, A. D., Willems, R. M. (2015). Simulating fiction: Individual differences in literature comprehension revealed with fMRI. *PLoS ONE, 10*(2), e0116492. doi:10.1371/journal.pone.0116492

Oatley, K. (2016). Fiction: Simulation of social worlds. *Trends in Cognitive Sciences, 20*(8), 618–628. doi: 10.1016/j.tics.2016.06.002

Ochsner, K. N., Ray, R. R., Hughes, B., McRae, K., Cooper, J. C., Weber, J., ... & Gross, J. J. (2009). Bottom-up and top-down processes in emotion generation common and distinct neural mechanisms. *Psychological Science, 20*(11), 1322–1331.

Olsson, C.-J., Jonsson, B., Larsson, A., & Nyberg, L. (2008). Motor representations and practice affect brain systems underlying imagery: An fMRI study of internal imagery in novices and active high jumpers. *The Open Neuroimaging Journal, 2*, 5–13.

Olsson, C. J., & Nyberg, L. (2010). Motor imagery: If you can't do it, you won't think it. *Scandinavian Journal of Medicine & Science in Sports, 20*(5), 711–715.

Olsson, C. J., & Nyberg, L. (2011). Brain simulation of action may be grounded in physical experience. *Neurocase, 17*(6), 501–505.

Pacherie, E., & Mylopoulos, M. (2020). Beyond automaticity: The psychological complexity of skill. *Topoi, 40*, 1–14.

Paris-Alemany, A., La Touche, R., Gadea-Mateos, L., Cuenca-Martínez, F., & Suso-Martí, L. (2019). Familiarity and complexity of a movement influences motor imagery in dancers: A cross-sectional study. *Scandinavian Journal of Medicine & Science in Sports, 29*(6), 897–906.

Pearson, J. (2019). The human imagination: The cognitive neuroscience of visual mental imagery. *Nature Reviews Neuroscience, 20*(10), 624–634.

Pearson, D. G., Deeprose, C., Wallace-Hadrill, S. M., Heyes, S. B., & Holmes, E. A. (2013). Assessing mental imagery in clinical psychology: A review of imagery measures and a guiding framework. *Clinical Psychology Review, 33*(1), 1–23.

Pecher, D., Zeelenberg, R., & Barsalou, L. W. (2003). Verifying different-modality properties for concepts produces switching costs. *Psychological Science, 14*(2), 119–124.

Pecher, D., Boot, I., & Van Dantzig, S. (2011). Abstract concepts: Sensory-motor grounding, metaphors, and beyond. In B. Ross (Ed.), *The psychology of learning and motivation* (Vol. 54, pp. 217–248). San Diego, CA: Academic Press.

Perkins, M. R. (1983). *Modal expressions in English*. London: Pinter.

Phillips, I., & Block, N. (2017). Debate on unconscious perception. In *Current controversies in philosophy of perception* (pp. 165–192). London and New York: Routledge.

Pressley, G. M. (1976). Mental imagery helps eight-year-olds remember what they read. *Journal of Educational Psychology, 68*(3), 355–359. doi:10.1037/0022-0663.68.3.355.

Prinz, J. (2010). When is perception conscious? In B. Nanay (Ed.), *Perceiving the world* (pp. 310–332). Oxford: Oxford University Press.

Prinz, J. (2015). Unconscious perception. In M. Matthen (Ed.), *Oxford handbook of philosophy of perception* (pp. 371–389). Oxford: Oxford University Press.

Pulvermüller, F. (2005). Brain mechanism linking language and action. *Nature Reviews Neuroscience, 6*(7), 576–582.

Pulvermüller, F., & Fadiga, L. (2010). Active perception: Sensorimotor circuits as a cortical basis for language. *Nature Reviews Neuroscience, 11*(5), 351–360.

Quirk, R., Greenbaum, S., Leech, G., & Svartvik, J. (1985). *A comprehensive grammar of the English language.* London: Longman.

Rall, J., & Harris, P. L. (2000). In Cinderella's slippers? Story comprehension from the protagonist's point of view. *Developmental Psychology, 36*(2), 202–208. doi:10.1037/0012-1649.36.2.202.

Rietveld, E., Denys, D., & van Westen, M. (2018). Ecological-Enactive Cognition as engaging with a field of relevant affordances. In A. Newen, L. De Bruin, & S. Gallagher (Eds.), *The Oxford handbook of 4E cognition* (pp. 41–70). Oxford: Oxford University Press.

Rowlands, M. (2010). *The new science of the mind: From extended mind to embodied phenomenology.* Cambridge, MA: MIT Press.

Rucińska, Z., & Gallagher, S. (2021). Making imagination even more embodied: Imagination, constraint and epistemic relevance. *Synthese, 199*, 1–28.

Rudy, J. W. (2008). *The neurobiology of learning and memory.* Sunderland, MA: Sinauer Associates.

Sandford, A. J., & Emmott, C. (2012). *Mind, brain and narrative.* Cambridge: Cambridge University Press.

Sadoski, M. (1983). An exploratory study of the relationships between reported imagery and the comprehension and recall of a story. *Reading Research Quarterly, 19*, 110–123.

Sadoski, M. (1985). The natural use of imagery in story comprehension and recall: Replication and extension. *Reading Research Quarterly, 20*, 658–667.

Sadoski, M., & Paivio, A. (2001). *Imagery and text: A dual coding theory of reading and writing.* New York and London: Routledge.

Scarry, E. (2001). *Dreaming by the book.* Princeton, NJ: Princeton University Press.

Scerrati, E., Baroni, G., Borghi, A. M., Galatolo, R., Lugli, L., & Nicoletti, R. (2015). The modality-switch effect: Visually and aurally presented prime sentences activate our senses. *Frontiers in Psychology, 6*, 1668.

Scerrati, E., Lugli, L., Nicoletti, R., & Borghi, A. M. (2016). The multilevel modality-switch effect: What happens when we see the bees buzzing and hear the diamonds glistening. *Psychonomic Bulletin & Review, 24*, 798–803. doi: 10.3758/s13423-016-1150-2

Schacter, D. L., & Addis, D. R. (2007). The cognitive neuroscience of constructive memory: Remembering the past and imagining the future. *Philosophical Transactions of the Royal Society B, 362*, 773–786. doi:10.1098/rstb.2007.2087

Schank, R. C., & Abelson, R. P. (1977). *Scripts, plans, goals, and understanding.* New York: Psychology Press.

Schilhab, T. S. (2002). Anthropomorphism and mental state attribution. *Animal Behaviour, 63*, 1021–1026.

Schilhab, T. S. (2007). Knowledge for real: On implicit and explicit representations and education. *Scandinavian Journal of Educational Research, 51*(3), 223–238.

Schilhab, T. S. (2011). Neural perspectives on "interactional expertise." *Journal of Consciousness Studies*, *18*(7–8), 99–116.

Schilhab, T. S. (2015a). Words as cultivators of others minds. *Frontiers in Psychology*, *6*, 1690.

Schilhab, T. S. (2015b). Doubletalk – The biological and social acquisition of language. *Biologically Inspired Cognitive Architectures*, *13*, 1–8.

Schilhab, T. S. (2015c). Why animals are not robots. *Phenomenology and the Cognitive Sciences*, *14*(3), 599–611.

Schilhab, T. S. (2017a). *Derived embodiment in abstract language*. Cham: Springer Verlag.

Schilhab, T. S. (2017b). Adaptive smart technology use: The need for meta-self-regulation. *Frontiers in Psychology*, *8*, 298.

Schilhab, T. S. (2018). Neural bottom-up and top-down processes in learning and teaching. *Postmodern Problems*, *8*(2), 228–245.

Schilhab, T. S., Balling, G., & Kuzmicova, A. (2018). Decreasing materiality from print to screen reading. *First Monday*, *10*.

Schilhab, T. S., Fridgeirsdottir, G., & Allerup, P. (2010). The midwife case: Do they "walk the talk"? *Phenomenology and the Cognitive Sciences*, *9*(1), 1–13.

Schilhab, T. S. & Walker, S. F. (2020). *Materiality of reading*. Aarhus: Aarhus University Press.

Schlochtermeier, L. H., Pehrs, C., Kappelhoff, H., Kuchinke, L., & Jacobs, A. M. (2015). Emotion processing in different media types: Realism, complexity, and immersion. *Journal of Systems and Integrative Neuroscience*, *1*, 41–47.

Schooler, J. W., Smallwood, J., Christoff, K., Handy, T. C., Reichle, E. D., & Sayette, M. A. (2011). Meta-awareness, perceptual decoupling and the wandering mind. *Trends in Cognitive Sciences*, *15*(7), 319–326.

Seilman, U., & Larsen, S. F. (1989). Personal resonance to literature: A study of remindings while reading. *Poetics*, *18*(1–2), 165–177.

Sheckley, B. G., & Bell, S. (2006). Experience, consciousness, and learning: Implications for instruction. *New Directions for Adult and Continuing Education*, *110*, 43.

Shepherd, J., & Mylopoulos, M. (2021). Unconscious perception and central coordinating agency. *Philosophical Studies*, 1–25.

Shusterman, R. (2009). Body consciousness and performance: Somaesthetics east and west. *Journal of Aesthetics and Art Criticism*, *67*(2), 133–145.

Simpson, P. (1993). *Language, ideology, and point of view*. London: Routledge.

Simpson, P. (2004). *Stylistics: A resource book for students*. London: Psychology Press.

Singer, T. (2006). The neuronal basis and ontogeny of empathy and mind reading: Review of literature and implications for future research. *Neuroscience and Biobehavioral Reviews*, *30*, 855–863.

Smallwood, J., McSpadden, M., & Schooler, J. W. (2008). When attention matters: The curious incident of the wandering mind. *Memory & Cognition*, *36*(6), 1144–1150.

Sood, A., & Jones, D. T. (2013). On mind wandering, attention, brain networks, and meditation. *Explore*, *9*(3), 136–141.

Sotirova, V. (2006). Reader responses to narrative point of view. *Poetics, 34*(2), 108–133.

Speed, L. J., & Majid, A. (2020). Grounding language in the neglected senses of touch, taste, and smell. *Cognitive Neuropsychology, 37*(5–6), 363–392.

Sternberg, M. (2003). Universals of narrative and their cognitivist fortunes (I). *Poetics Today, 24,* 297–395.

Stockwell, P. (2002). *Cognitive poetics: An introduction.* London: Routledge.

Strick, M., van Noorden, T. H., Ritskes, R. R., de Ruiter, J. R., & Dijksterhuis, A. (2012). Zen meditation and access to information in the unconscious. *Consciousness and Cognition, 21*(3), 1476–1481.

Thalbourne, M. A. (2000). Transliminality and creativity. *Journal of Creative Behavior, 34*(3), 193–202.

Thalbourne, M. A. (2009). Transliminality, anomalous belief and experience, and hypnotisability. *Australian Journal of Clinical & Experimental Hypnosis, 37*(2), 119–130.

Toner, J., & Moran, A. (2011). The effects of conscious processing on golf putting proficiency and kinematics. *Journal of Sports Sciences, 29*(7), 673–683.

Trasmundi, S. B., Kokkola, L., Schilhab, T., & Mangen, A. (2021). A distributed perspective on reading: Implications for education. *Language Sciences, 84,* 101367.

Uspensky, B. A. (1972). Structural isomorphism of verbal and visual art. *Poetics, 2*(1), 5–39. doi:10.1016/0304-422x(72)90028-9.

van Sommers, P. (1984). *Drawing and cognition: Descriptive and experimental studies of graphics production and processes.* Cambridge: Cambridge University Press.

Varga, S., & Heck, D. H. (2017). Rhythms of the body, rhythms of the brain: Respiration, neural oscillations, and embodied cognition. *Consciousness and Cognition, 56,* 77–90.

Verdonk, P. (2002). Perspectives on meaning. In *Stylistics* (pp. 29–40). New York: Oxford University Press.

Vitali, F., Tarperi, C., Cristini, J., Rinaldi, A., Zelli, A., Lucidi, F., ... & Robazza, C. (2019). Action monitoring through external or internal focus of attention does not impair endurance performance. *Frontiers in Psychology, 10,* 535.

Walter, S. (2009). Locked-in syndrome, BCI, and a confusion about embodied, embedded, extended, and enacted cognition. *Neuroethics, 3*(1), 61–72. doi:10.1007/s12152-009-9050-z.

Willems, R. M., & Casasanto, D. (2011). Flexibility in embodied language understanding. *Frontiers in Psychology, 2,* 116.

Wilson, M. (2002). Six views of embodied cognition. *Psychonomic Bulletin & Review, 9*(4), 625–636.

Zwaan, R. A. (1999). Situation models. *Current Directions in Psychological Science, 8*(1), 15–18. doi:10.1111/1467-8721.00004.

Zwaan, R. A. (2009). Mental simulation in language comprehension and social cognition. *European Journal of Social Psychology, 39,* 1142–1150. doi:10.1002/ejsp.661

Zwaan, R. A., & Madden, C. J. (2005). Embodied sentence comprehension. In D. Pecher & R. A. Zwaan (Eds.), *Grounding cognition: The role of perception and action in memory, language, and thinking* (pp. 224–245). Cambridge: Cambridge University Press.

Zwaan, R. A., Stanfield, R. A., & Yaxley, R. H. (2002). Language comprehenders mentally represent the shapes of objects. *Psychological Science, 13*(2), 168–171.

Index

For Product Safety Concerns and Information please contact our EU
representative GPSR@taylorandfrancis.com
Taylor & Francis Verlag GmbH, Kaufingerstraße 24, 80331 München, Germany

9 781032 125916